DrawBridge

Caitlin Press Inc.
8100 Alderwood Road,
Halfmoon Bay, BC V0N 1Y1
www.caitlin-press.com

Text design by Gerilee McBride Design
Cover design by Vici Johnstone
Edited by Christine Savage
Printed in Canada

Caitlin Press Inc. acknowledges financial support from the Government of Canada
and the Canada Council for the Arts, and the Province of British Columbia through
the British Columbia Arts Council and the Book Publisher's Tax Credit.

Library and Archives Canada Cataloguing in Publication

Title: DrawBridge : drawing alongside my brother's schizophrenia / author, Joan Boxall ;
illustrated by Stephen A. Corcoran.
Names: Boxall, Joan, 1954– author. | Corcoran, Stephen A., 1948–2013, illustrator.

Description: Includes bibliographical references.

Identifiers: Canadiana 20190050209 | ISBN 9781773860022 (softcover)

Subjects: LCSH: Corcoran, Stephen A., 1948–2013. | LCSH: Corcoran, Stephen A., 1948–
2013—Mental health. | LCSH: Corcoran, Stephen A., 1948-2013—Family. | LCSH: Boxall,
Joan, 1954-—Family. | LCSH: Schizophrenia and the arts. | LCSH: Art and mental illness.
| LCSH: Artists with mental disabilities—Canada—Biography. | LCSH: Schizophrenics—
Canada—Biography. | LCSH: Schizophrenics—Family relationships—Canada.

Classification: LCC RC514 .B69 2019 | DDC 616.89/80092—dc23

DrawBridge

Drawing Alongside
My Brother's Schizophrenia

By **JOAN BOXALL**
Illustrations by **STEPHEN A. CORCORAN**

CAITLIN PRESS

Your drawing should be an expression of your spiritual sight...
Draw not a line, but an inspired line...
A line expresses your pride, fear and hope...
Yours should be the drawing of the human spirit through the
human form...
Search for the simple constructive forces, like the lines of a
suspension bridge.[1]

—*Robert Henri (1865–1929)*
American painter and inspired teacher

CONTENTS

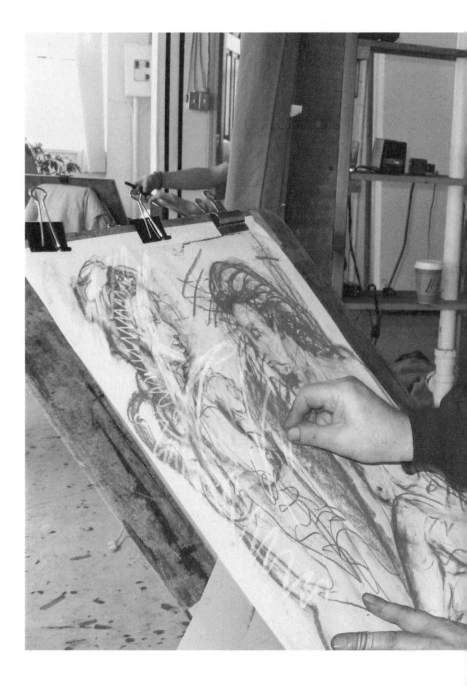

Stephen A. Corcoran at work.

Stephen A. Corcoran pondering a day's work, June 2008.

FOREWORD

*By Gillian Siddall, president and vice-chancellor
of Emily Carr University of Art + Design*

DRAWBRIDGE TELLS THE poignant story of the author's complex journey of renewing her relationship with her estranged brother through making art together. Joan Boxall's brother, Stephen Corcoran, lived with schizophrenia, and they went many years without seeing much of each other. When Joan decides to make a concerted effort to reconnect with him in middle age, the challenges of their interactions with each other resolve in unexpected and beautiful ways when they begin to take drawing classes together at the Art Studios in Vancouver, whose mandate is to support mental health and addiction recovery through art making. Without being sentimental, the book demonstrates how powerfully making art can connect people, can make community and can give voice to someone like Stephen, who was otherwise socially marginalized by his illness. Stephen finds some measure of peace when making art, and Joan finds a renewed and profound appreciation for her brother and the tremendous struggles he has faced throughout his life. His work culminated in two solo shows in Vancouver.

After his death, Joan established the Stephen A. Corcoran Memorial Award at the Emily Carr University of Art + Design, which Stephen attended in the 1960s when it was called the Vancouver School of Art. The award supports students dealing with mental health issues and is a testament to Stephen's strength and creativity, as well as the powerful roles that art and art making can play in our lives.

APOLOGIA

AN APOLOGIA IS NOT an apology. It expresses no wrongdoing. Rather, it is an explanation, from the Greek expression "in defence of"— in this case, an attempt to sidestep societal censure around a chronic mental illness. A quick and loose sketch, done freehand for what was seen and left unseen, vis-à-vis drawing mediums, such as myself.

My brother Steve and I are about to connect some dots. We are middle-aged siblings. Middle age as a place in time was the Middle-earth that J.R.R. Tolkien wrote about in *The Hobbit*[2], one of Steve's beloved folk tales—a place where humans lived and interacted. Middle age has brought us to a divide. Once the earthen divide is levelled, we draw closer.

Dot connection comes later, as Steve Jobs said: "You can't connect the dots looking forward; you can only connect them looking backwards....Believing that the dots will connect down the road will give you the confidence to follow your heart even when it leads you off the well-worn path, and that will make all the difference."[3]

Even though I'm looking backwards, I embark on my ramble with Steve in a present tense: a kind of tensor-bandage awareness. I invite the reader to wear its tautness with me: to be aware in our moments together. What difference that makes, you be the judge.

Some names have been changed to protect privacy. Some have been created to connect dots. Here come the dotty dots, the pixie pixels, the didgeridoodles.

Steve and I remain, faithfully yours.

CHAPTER 1

Sharpie

STEVE AND I EMBODY two separate circles. Like unicyclists, we roll forward and back, feeling our balance. *Pivot, pivot, bump.* Two wheels slide into a familial frame. *Ker-clunk.*

My fifty years to his fifty-five. In family-constellation studies, Steve is an insider and I am an outsider, at number three and number six of seven birth-order positions. Steve, as third child and soon thereafter middle child, isn't predetermined to be a black sheep.

Sociologist and medical historian Peter Morrell says that third children like Steve "understand how people operate in social groups fairly intuitively because that is pretty well what they have been forced into doing since birth. They have sound intuition, understand clearly how groups operate, fit in well with teams and work well with others."[4]

I was one of two afterthoughts (even though my mother claimed that none of us were planned). In terms of birth order, number sixes are undocumented. Besides, stellar points you're born into aren't ones of your choosing. Star constellations don't last. They run out of fuel. They explode, or implode. The shock waves are felt over time.

The two of us turn out, unwittingly, to be like *The Simpsons* clan: I am little sister Lisa to his Bart. Contrary to the popular animated television series, I am no genius. Neither is Steve the rebel he makes himself out to be. They, *The Simpsons*, become Steve's pseudo-family. He hangs with them longer than he hung with us. Their dysfunction makes everything else okay.

※

We are an unlikely match for sibling reunification. Many dots in our history expand to make gaps. The time gap (our age difference). The gender gap (five boys and two girls). The household gap (the top-floor bedrooms were for the girls, and the basement for the boys). My sister and I shared Mum and Dad's main-floor bathroom and tub. The boys had a tin-can shower across from the furnace. Off to bed for the younger ones while the older ones watched TV in the downstairs rec room.

We ate in two shifts (the meal gap). Younger brother Fred and I ate with Mum and Dad first; the remaining five chowed down afterwards in quick succession. We were the "seagulls"; Dad coined the term for the greed and speed of our appetites. Mealtimes later became flextimes where the older ones might not show up.

When I was born, Steve was five and a half, nearly school age. By the time I was in elementary school, he was in high school, and by the time I got there, he'd graduated. Shortly thereafter, Steve left home. I'd had a decade to get to know him, but it wasn't to be then. It is to be now.

Take it piecemeal. Here we are on our respective unicycles.

※

Steve: ready for his doctor's appointment. Getting ready has taken three hours. Maybe three days. I say "maybe" because this is supposition. He knows where he's going: what he has to do.

Mum always sang that old Irish folk song "I Know Where I'm Going," so I guess we come by it naturally.

There are groceries to get, and reading materials. There's the bank, scrabbling a meal together, and the appointment around which it all rotates, once a month. I can just picture it...

Dr. P for Pearce. Once he's seen the doc, he'll skewer the shopping kebab.

Steve's thinking, "Why not put Dr. P on the kebab. Hear him squeal."

He whistles his way out the front door, locking the inner door and then the outer. He emits a piggy squeal betwixt the two. He's creating a mobile comic strip—building scenarios as he ambles to the bus stop, pulling his buggy behind him.

"Examining your train of thought, Doc. After that, I'll shove a banana up your ass. Maybe some money after that, and a comic book. Do you have a light? Some embalming fluid?"

Steve lets off steam in hopes he won't have any left when he gets there. He keeps up a running diatribe, mezza voce, especially when he has him-selves around—the ones who visit his psyche at any given moment. On and off buses. Into the building. Into the wait room. In between times.

Steve shows Dr. P highlighted readings from a magazine he's picked up in a book bin. This, his latest fixation: "No praise, no blame. Buddhist equilibrium," Steve says to the doc, and later on to me, more than once.

"Carl Jung brought it to psychology," says Dr. P. "What do praise and blame mean to you?"

"Staying passive. Pacifist...in a sack."

"Tell me more," says Dr. P.

"Flat, fat. Apathetic, pathetic...same old, same diff," says Steve.

American Buddhist nun Pema Chodron refers to praise and blame as two of eight dharmas, which are loosely translated as the "right way of living." She says, "Peace is…the well-being that comes when we see the infinite pairs of opposites as complementary."[5]

My theory is that opposites drift into oneness once we die. Our bodies provide a certain point of view: inward and outward. Who cares about tall or short, fat or thin, opinionated or not, once we are spirits? Until then, Pema's concept of complementary pairs brings cohesion.

She goes on to say: "We have a lot of opinions, and we tend to take them as truth. But actually they aren't truth. They are just our opinions…judgmental or critical…nothing more or less."[6]

"Here are my opinions, Pema et al.," offer I on my recollections. Grounded in assurance, this is the sum of my reality, with some imaginary stretches: based on being immersed with Steve one day a week for a decade.

⁂

Steve's looking for relief from negative dharmas—pain, blame, disgrace and loss. He's looking for some peace—of mind.

Owning actions is part of free will. The aftermath of a choice might be praise, or it might be its blameful underbelly. Who measures a good or bad choice? Society members? Social philosophers? Parents? A sister like me?

Mental illness alters judgment. When weighed on a moral scale, sound minds make reasonably sound judgments. Once mental stability is disabled, dis-ability impairs and plugs a negative prefix onto the approval rating. Dis is an insult or an affront.

Bad enough for him, bad enough for me, his little dis-sis.

Bad son. Bad brother. Bad husband. Bad father. Is that what Steve is? Or is that his opinion (and possibly mine) of who he is?

Praise is easier to shake off, like fluff. For Steve, praise and blame look alike. It comes down to whether anyone gives credence to what others think. Approving and reproving opinions emanate from others, or perceived others. Steve is wary of opinions.

When I ask him over for a meal, he asks, "Oh, is that a dinner party?" I can tell from his tone, he's not coming. "Sort of," I say.

"Where people toss around opinions? No thanks, Joan," he says.

I guess he's saying, "Your world observations are not mine, your generally held views are not mine," and ultimately, "Your reality is not mine." Early on, our dots are not connecting.

%

"More lithium, Steve?" asks Dr. P.

"No."

"Next month, then? I'll be back from China," says Dr. P.

"Okay. Have fun," Steve says as he tucks the magazine into his buggy and leaves Dr. P's office. The ultraviolet light flickers. Something invokes Steve's companions—Bart, Bilbo and Clown.

Does he hear them first? Or see them? Do they emanate from within? Either way, they appear as he exits onto the street. Their showing up is never a shock. He recognizes, even welcomes them. The recognition may be more auditory than visual. They are his good voices, on a good day, of which this is one.

%

If I ask Steve about his voices and visions I am trespassing. He's lived with them for so long; they are his covert friends. For him, they are real—his and his alone. I'm not privy to whether they are constant or temporary.

"Mind your own business, Joan," he says.

Nowadays, I no longer follow that advice. I investigate using a quasi-scientific method. I ask questions, do research, form hypotheses, draw conclusions. Trouble is this experiment is non-reproducible. It is a siblings' test case.

I'm going to trespass. I'm going to conjecture. I'm about to make some educated guesses. Studies have shown there's a lot of truth in knowledgeable guesses. Perhaps some scientifically curious minds will take it further—second opinions, if you will.

Dr. John Nash, a Nobel Prize winner and schizophrenia sufferer, said, "You're really talking to yourself is what the voices are, but it's also parallel to a dream. In a dream it's typical not to be rational."[7]

Here are the preliminary results.

///

"Just answer the question, Corky," says Ken.

To my husband, I am Corky or Cork. He is an ex-Brit, with a liking for cockney nicknames. My dad was Corky to my mum and to friends—a pet name for Corcoran, my Irish surname.

"Remind me what it was?" I raise my most charming smile and less-than-charming eyebrows.

"When you want to go skiing," Ken says.

He's home with the groceries, and I've cleaned kitchen and bathrooms on a Saturday-chores morning in February: damp and rainy, but cold enough for snow higher up on the cross-country slopes. Skies are grey through curtainless windows. Up here on the side of a mountain, it's a temperate-rainforest morning that curtains our world.

We live on the edge, tucked under Grouse Mountain, a half-hour drive from Nordic skiing at Hollyburn Ridge. Cloud and drizzle, the perfect backdrop for a funeral—yet fresh air, brightness and whiteness seem livelier.

"The memorial is on my mind."

"It's a week away," says Ken.

"I'll miss Tuesdays with Mum and Dad."

"She's been gone over a year," Ken says.

"Dad was a week in hospital before passing. Mum, a whole year in a nursing home. She was better at adapting…"

"Your dad in a nursing home?" Ken says. "That was never going to happen."

"Yeah, fiercely independent…both of them in a better place now. Speaking of better places, let's ski after brunch."

※

"Come on," Steve says to Bart, Bilbo and Clown.

They're busing to the bank. When Steve gets on, passengers move to seats farther back. Strangers sidestep this dishevelled man who's talking to himself. Stigma.

Stigma stems from the Greek word "stigmata"—a reference to the wounds of the crucified Christ. Social stigma is a mark of disgrace that sticks to the mentally ill like gum to the bottom of a shoe. Steve is the only one aware that he's got company. That makes strangers skittish.

Steve sits up front, near the bus driver, with his imaginary friends. He tries not to giggle at what they're saying. I've heard him stifle giggles many a time. That they entertain him is some comfort.

"Only crazy people hear voices," Steve tells me. That's his way of saying, "Don't bring it up, Joan." He clams up if I notice him speaking to them, yet I have an inkling of who they are. You may well ask how that is possible. Is it sensitivity, receptivity or both?

※

I get hay fever, more aptly named rhinitis, for its year-round runny nose. In my case, itchy eyes and irritated sinuses react to mould, dust mites and cat dander (not merely hay or ragweed). I once babysat a family with five Siamese (cats, not children). When the parents came home, I kept up a Cheshire-cat smile to hide my swollen, red eyes.

Adding insult to allergen, throw in eczema, food allergies and tree pollen irritation. As a kid, I stayed indoors in hay-fever season while my brothers mowed the lawn. My chores were indoor ones: dusting and vacuuming—crazy for a kid with dust and pollen allergies, but sharing chores was a household work ethic. Mum and Dad didn't recognize the perennial nature of my allergies.

"Stay in the backyard," was Dad's solution.

I sang songs Mum taught me, like "Que Será, Será." Good enough for Doris Day—good enough for Mum and me. The future of what would be seemed as distant as what lay beyond the backyard's green picket fence of protectiveness.

One dermatologist suggests I might be made this way. This diagnosis infuriates me. "That wasn't a treatment; it was an accusation," I say to Ken when I get home. Instead of getting on top of my skin, the specialist gets under it.

Extreme cases are HSPs or highly sensitive people. They pick up on vibes or energy fields. I sniff things out—way beyond the daily pollen count. HSPs are empaths, part chameleon. Wary of labels, they soak up other people's colours, moods and needs. It's hard to stop a sponge doing what it does. They are, as researcher and natural-born empath Christel Broederlow describes them, "poets in motion.... The artistic community [is] filled with [these] listeners of life."[8]

Psychologists Elaine and Arthur Aron[9] coined HSP in the 1990s for people who are wired a bit more deeply—people whose personality trait applies to 20 percent of a still-not-well-understood population.

Middle-distance running in my early teens and twenties boosted my immune system. I hopped the green picket fence: running laps of a track, up and down field hockey wings and along the Stanley Park seawall and trails. I rode my bicycle to local tournaments and track meets. No better antihistamine than the adrenalin shot of a starter's pistol or an umpire's whistle. I took up Nordic skiing and ocean kayaking. Being on the ocean or snow minimized my allergic reactions. These were the quiet spaces an HSP needs, away from the crowd.

Becoming an athlete, a teacher, a nature lover, a singer, a poet and a traveller fostered an interest in "the Other" that journalist Ryszard Kapuściński talked and wrote about in a compilation of lectures.[10] A world-renowned Polish journalist, Kapuściński was interested in the tug-of-war between humanity and the tribal dictates of who's in and who's out. In an interview, he described his own writing as a "combination of three elements...exploration...reading...reflection."[11] Those three elements ooze out in my travelogues, blogs and poems. Ken and I travel for a month in summer, or on my teaching breaks: to Mayan temples in Mexico or across Hawaiian calderas; tuning our eyes and ears to Costa Rican wildlife or exploring history and prehistory in England and France; bicycle or kayak touring. I read and reflect in musings that end up in a local lifestyle magazine.

Steve listens to my edited travel tales. Edited because I don't want to confound him with too much information, yet I want him to know where I go, when I'll be away. He wears a tee-shirt memento I've given him of cave paintings from Lascaux, France. His tee is an aurochs in motion, an early ancestor of cows. In return, he brings me an article on Lucy, the 3.2-million-year-old Ethiopian skeleton— our first up-standing citizen. We're both curious about our roots.

Cave artists purportedly used the contours of candlelit cave walls to bring a third dimension (3-D) to their work. As the candles flickered, the deliria of working in a sensory-deprived state set the hunt in motion. They were the first animators. Mineral pigments and charcoals depict equines, stags and bulls in hunting rituals going back tens of thousands of years. Steve and I will soon use similar tools to make art.

Steve stun guns me with prolonged soliloquies. It takes all my inquisitive intuition to read him. It's not purely an HSP's empath fatigue at the end of a day with Steve. My system overloads, until I return from Tuesday-night choral singing sessions, saturated in healing overtones.

While figuring him out, I keep sticking my nose in it. He rubs in my shortfalls. Being sensitive makes me an easy mark, yet sniffing things out has curious advantages. I get into my brother's shoes.

"Flower your empathy,"[12] says social philosopher Roman Krznaric, as an acid test of brotherly love.

It is as if Steve positions a two-way mirror between us. Two-ways have a small gap between the reflection and the object being reflected. A small but not insurmountable gap allows the viewer to observe without detection…they're also called one-ways, as there's only one way a person can be seen—from the darker to the brighter side.

The interaction that Steve and I are about to share isn't the usual two-way—it isn't in an interrogation room with soundproof glass. No detective, no criminal. We are in this together, and in order to know each other, the gap between us must evaporate.

Auditory hallucinations are gap creators. If Steve does see his imaginary friends, before long, they blend into a surround-sound presence, blocking out reality. He feels their presence. This HSP can picture it.

※

"Aren't your kids from China?" says Bart, of Simpson family fame.

"They're Hawaiian, you dumb fuck," says Steve.

"Watch your lingo, amigo," says the bus driver, glaring into his rear-view mirror.

"You can borrow my ring and go with Doc if you want," offers Bilbo.

"That's okay," says Steve.

"We are Siamese if you please," says Clown.

"Shut the fuck up," says Steve. The bus driver swings open the door.

"This is where you get out, pal," says the bus driver.

Steve's been shown the door before. This time, he's conveniently one stop shy of the bank. He joins the lineup while the three amigos—Bart, Bilbo and Clown—wait outside. They're good at waiting.

He withdraws enough cash to order pizza next door, using a coupon that he takes five minutes to find in one of his many cargo-pant pockets. Day-old bread is another bargain to be had. Steve walks as if there is no time to spare. The faster he goes, the less stigma time. The last thing to bungee on top of the buggy is the pizza box before he reuses his bus transfer ten more stops west.

The hallucinations walk on and off unnoticed. Noticeable is Steve's self-chat.

※

I live off Vancouver's grid, on the North Shore above the Capilano reservoir. Ken and I joke that it's overseas: over the Lions Gate Bridge, a long way for Vancouverites, some say, given traffic tie-ups and transit snarls.

Steve is in the Sunset area of Vancouver's southeast, which borders Oakridge to the west and Victoria-Fraserview to the east. Like contradictory compass readings, we align southeast and north-west. Our geographic opposition is in perfect disaccord.

The difference in rainfall between the North Shore and Metro Vancouver is just as pivotal: the higher and farther north one goes, the more rain. Steve's Sunset neighbourhood gets half the annual rainfall of North Vancouver. He lives on the sunny side, near a designated bicycle artery that connects our north-south polarity. This is our two-way—I peer from the dark cloud canopy of the North Shore to Vancouver's clarity. Yet mental illness clouds his outlook. As a result, we each have a shrouded, yet relative, view of the other.

※

Steve loves bicycles, but buggies carry more. He exits the bus and wheels his cart down a nearby laneway. Having never driven a car or flown in an airplane, he has a small eco-footprint.

We try the SkyTrain once; it makes him nervous. The Aquabus transports tourists to and from Granville Island Public Market around False Creek. Again, once was enough. In the car with me, he snaps the seat belt several times before takeoff. Technology has raced these past twenty years of his isolation. He hasn't kept pace.

※

Bart, Bilbo and Clown—Steve's straggly trio—kick along.

Bart Simpson is the ten-year-old fictional rebel from *The Simpsons* television series. The childish one. Bilbo Baggins is J.R.R. Tolkien's wannabe wise man. A middle-aged hobbit and part-time burglar, he goes on an odyssey. Clown is the slapstick one who doesn't care. Steve plays each one like a voice-over actor. I've heard them all, from time to time, when Steve impersonates the "child," the "wise man" or the "clown."

Of the three clown types, Marcel Marceau plays Bip the Clown in a mime called the "art of silence." Steve finds the silence he craves when he plays a mute whiteface.

Krusty the Clown is the red-nosed buffoon type who hosts Bart and Lisa Simpson's favourite television show. Krusty wears mismatched accessories that mirror Steve's look, particularly his many styles of glasses, moustaches, beards and haircuts. Steve's a do-it-yourself Mr. Potato Head kind of guy.

The third clown type wears tattered tramp clothing with grease-painted skin, like Red Skelton's Freddy the Freeloader[13]. Tramps monologue and perform juggling, magic and art tricks.

Steve tries his hand at all clown types. They are the friends who come to his side—his faithful thought disorders.

Cubism was a Picasso-Braque artistic movement of the early twentieth century. The movement abandoned a single viewpoint, and it parallels Steve's points of view. Some are his. Some he voices. Some he hears. Others he sees, in a fashion. It all gets stuck...on the collage of Steve's disjointed thoughts.

※

Steve pulls his buggy around the side of the house and up the front stairs. He pulls out a key ring, opens two glass-paned doors and pulls the cart to the base of the interior stairs. He lifts the cart up twenty stairs. He rents the upstairs, but his belongings drift onto the stairs and stairwell, and along the entranceway and hallway.

Possessions are dear to those who suffer loss. To those who have difficulty focusing, regulating emotion or decision-making, collecting fills the gap. Thrift may be part of it. All are part of Steve's parcels. Part. And parcel.

Holding on is comforting. Holding on quells fear. Holding on holds us up.

First glance tells you this house is tidy. Look again. Peeling white-with-blue-trim paint. Cracked windowpanes. The front steps sway in an unhinged state. Visible from the street is the glassed-in veranda and its contents, a mishmash of bicycle parts, hanging or stacked on shelves: tires, hubs, frames. Dust and grime repel intruders. Behind the facade, tiers teeter.

Steve spins one of five rusty bicycle wheels hanging in the front entrance and taps a bicycle frame.

Tap, tap. Spin, spin. "Need another one," he says.

"We passed some bicycle parts in the lane yesterday," says Bart.

"No room today, Coffee Can, maybe tomorrow."

Steve balances books and groceries on the pizza box as he climbs the cluttered stairwell, turning on the landing's last five stairs. He leaves the buggy and his pals below; they are fading auras and aural sounds in the dim light. Clearing space on the bed, he eats a slice while looking at a graphic novel he picked up in a free-book bin. He puts on a second pair of glasses (overtop of the first). He gets up to open the iced-over fridge, takes a can of beer from the door, pulls the tab, takes a long swig, props himself against a grubby pillow, leafs through one of the books, pops a lithium, takes another swig and then falls asleep, fully clothed.

///

I glide out onto the cross-country ski track with Ken. It is a wonderland of light, silky snow tracks. Legs and arms keep measure. In the gaps, there is time for reflection.

///

Sharpies are drawing tools for artistic rendering. They are felt markers with fine, chiselled tips. Black and permanent. Such is the severity of Steve's minimally medicated schizophrenia.

The creators of Sharpies adapted a variety of tips—some erasable, some retractable.

Former Canadian astronaut Chris Hadfield, of the International Space Station, likes how they function in space "any which way and... still work."[14]

My brother is about to tip and draw out his figurative Sharpie— his adaptability put to the test.

Mine, too.

///

I.D.

When will I see myself as I truly am?

Stripped down semblance—

Serene, composed, tranquil.

Turn, spin, evolve.

Dizzy the coil.

Obscure turmoil.

CHAPTER 2

Conté

DARREN IS A YEAR and four months Steve's elder. Brothers. He pulls up outside Steve's place, carrying a dark suit under Cellophane. He pounds on the front door. "Steve?"

The doorbell doesn't work. I've been there when Darren announces his arrival in this way. It is effective.

"Be right there," Steve shouts back. He picks his way downstairs over stacks of books, newspapers and magazines.

"Pretty cluttered," Darren says. Darren relays this exchange to me later on.

"MYOB—for bullshit," says Steve.

"It's a fire hazard, Steve. Lawrence lives here too. He's the owner. Clean it up."

"How'd you like me to snafu your stuff?" says Steve.

"Tomorrow's Dad's funeral; here's a suit. There's a shirt and tie inside. I'll pick you up at ten."

"Dead people's clothing?" (I wince, hearing Darren's account of Steve's reference to Dad.)

"They're clean, Steve. They'll fit you."

Lawrence appears from the hallway. Darren and Lawrence went to the same high school and lifted weights together in Darren's makeshift weight room in our family garage. Later on, Lawrence took Steve in as a tenant.

"Hey, Lawrence, how's it going?"

"Good, Darren. Sorry to read your dad's obit in the newspaper."

"Thanks, Lawrence. We'll have lunch before too long, eh?" Darren says. To Steve, Darren says, "See you tomorrow. Ten o'clock."

///

Steve sits in a pew at the back of St. John the Apostle Roman Catholic Church. He is restless but lasts through the service; he sits next to Rod, our eldest brother, who's arrived from the eastern United States for the funeral. Father Bob leads the service. I do a reading, a bit wobbly, but blurt it out. Sally and my younger brother, Fred, each do a fine job of reading. Steve hasn't been in a church since Mum died in 2002, a year and two months earlier. He does a fine job of sitting still.

"Give him, O Lord, your peace and may eternal light shine upon him," says Father Bob.

"Amen," we intone.

This is the church of our childhoods. This is the church we walked to and from every Sunday—three blocks gently downhill and three blocks back up. This is the church where I had my first communion, my first folk mass solo, my first confessions to lying and swearing (the easiest sins to account for) and my first faint from the fasting rule of no breakfast. This is the church where Father Bob, one of my brothers, married Ken and me.

This sombre day matches the dark wood interior, that same dark wood interior of our childhood home on a shady Trafalgar corner in a neighbourhood where the streets are named for English battles (Carnarvon, Blenheim, Waterloo, Balaclava, Dunbar) and trees (Arbutus, Elm, Balsam, Larch, Yew). Battles and trees have brought us to our knees.

In mourning and in celebrating Dad, what could become a delusional trigger for Steve does not.

Three potentialities could trigger psychosis this day: stress, religion and emotion. The preventives are that this celebration has been well thought out. Not much stress. Dad's death is not unexpected. Neither is our family highly emotional. As for religion, Steve has long ago dismissed the voices he hears as God's.

"Whose voice is it? A spy who's implanted a chip in my brain?" Steve might once have thought.

Steve has distanced himself from the emotional pressures that religion and family can evoke. In this way, the triggers elude him.

Even though Darren's home is walking distance from the church, we drive from the memorial to the wake. At a traditional wake, mourners console the family and view the deceased. The viewing is over. Dad's been cremated. At Darren's, people offer condolences over drinks and snacks. I scan the room. Steve is in a corner, in a monologue with Darren's wife. I see a former next-door neighbour.

"Hi Helen, nice to see you. Do you still live in the old neighbourhood?"

"Oh no. I'm in a Kerrisdale apartment now," says Helen. Kerrisdale is the name of our old neighbourhood, so I know Helen hasn't moved far. "If you don't mind me saying, Joan...someone has to help Steve," Helen adds.

"Yes. Darren and I are his trustees."

"No, I mean, really help him...somehow," says Helen.

Dad and Darren arranged a trust for Steve in Dad's will. After Dad's death, Darren asks me to be a second trustee, a checkmate to account for Steve's gift from our parents: to help manage Steve's inheritance.

A trust is an arrangement in which cash is held for someone, to be spent under certain conditions, for certain things. I don't see myself as a money manager, but Darren is good with numbers. "Keep the receipts, Joan," Darren said. "Steve can afford to buy what he needs."

Helen's question resonates with me: How am I going to really help Steve?

Helen lived with her elderly parents and aunt while working full-time. Her words have meaning, although I'm not quite sure what.

After the memorial and refreshments, Darren takes Steve home.

"I'll pick up the suit next week, Steve," says Darren.

I'll see Steve next week too, but will I be able to help him? Really help him?

※

As a *Mad Magazine* fan, Steve was headed for art school. His cartoons were in the high school newspaper. Parody shaped Steve's sense of humour. The *Mad Magazine* mascot, Alfred E. Neuman, lampooned everything from religion and politics to social standing. Alfred's face appeared on every *Mad* cover, and his features transmuted into any number of celebs, from King Kong to Batman, and from Michael Jackson to the Maharishi, Mona Lisa, George W. Bush and Harry Potter. Steve read every issue. He became that satirical humourist that questioned authority while laughing at it. That became the mode in *Saturday Night Live* and *The Simpsons* as well. In the last twenty-five years, kids have grown up with Harry Potter; Steve grew up with Alfred E.[15]

"Look out, Disney," I thought. "Steve will have his own animated feature one day."

Instead, animated shorts come to him daily, hourly. Unsolicited.

Steve left home at eighteen. I have a foggy memory of him and Dad arguing. Steve's wild mane of reddish-gold curls. Dad's hair: jet black, barber cut and slicked back with Vitalis Hair Tonic. Steve wanting independence. Dad shouting that working at a sawmill wasn't a real @#$% job, or any kind of @#$% independence. Steve didn't back down. He'd work and pay his way...for art classes. He grabbed a backpack and headed out the door.

Steve had been smoking weed. Even I knew that he'd had a pot plant growing in his closet. Whether he harvested his own or bought it with pocket money, I didn't know.

In a 2018 *Maclean's* magazine article, Joe Castaldo reports that "those who smoke regularly double their risk of reporting psychotic symptoms or being diagnosed with schizophrenia in adulthood....Long-term use is also associated with problems in attention, memory, impulse control, problem solving and emotional regulation...[affecting] the very makeup of the brain, which is still developing in youth."[16]

The Canadian Centre on Substance Abuse and Addiction announced that evidence is mounting on the impact of cannabis on the teen brain. The Canadian Medical Association recommends its use for a post-adolescent brain. But in the late 1960s, my parents had no idea what was going on.

Mum found a stash, cleaning out Steve's empty lunch box, the kind with a Thermos in the lid.

"Steve, you didn't eat your granola," she called downstairs. (The baggie of granola was marijuana. We found that hilarious at the time.)

"I never wanted Steve to leave home," Dad admitted in his later years.

Mum and Dad were ill-prepared to deal with the hippie revolution. They'd dealt with a world war, but to a younger generation they were squares. To the squares they were hippies, yet the hippies called themselves freaks. What a freaking divide—what an almighty gap.

Sometime in the next few years Steve had a psychotic break, which wasn't a breakthrough—more like a fracture in reasoning skills. Mum and Dad thought he'd hit his head, maybe gotten into a fight. In actuality, he had begun a fight—one that would be of, and for, his lifetime.

Between working at the mill, studying at the Vancouver School of Art, training as a welder, living communally, getting married and attempting to raise two sons, Steve's artistic quest stalled. The seasonal jobs of tree planting and picking mushrooms (and testing them) abstracted him. He lost his livelihood, his family and his dream.

※

I left home at twenty-two to live off campus and finish off one more year of studies at UBC before teaching physical education and English in small-town British Columbia. I returned to Vancouver two years later; met Ken at the YMCA running club; taught English, French and physical education; and coached field hockey and track. Once my hip sockets began to rot with osteoarthritis, I retrained at a local community college to teach English to adults (ESL).

My job redirection coincided with our wedding, with Ken selling his business and with our subsequent health challenges: my right and left total hip replacements and Ken's colon cancer and subsequent chemotherapy. We cut meat from our diets and moved from Vancouver to the North Shore, our healing place.

Part-time teaching freed Tuesday time for me to help out with my aging parents and then with Steve.

I liked teaching adult beginners of English. Learning French prepared me for teaching English: the greetings, the grammar, the steadfast build of vocabulary and syntax. Language learning put me in the learner's seat. Appreciating my students' frustrations equipped me to be their guide.

The physicality of physical-education training overlapped into classroom body-language antics. Songs fit into a flexible curriculum. I compiled and recorded a tape of songs to help English learners, *Joan's Jam*. I workshopped it with student teachers, teachers and students.

※

Prior to my decade with Steve was a decade of Tuesdays with Mum and Dad. Dad fixed cheese-and-tomato sandwiches with sweet pickles. I'd change linens, do laundry and watch comedy reruns with them. Classics from the 1950s filled their afternoons: *All in the Family, I Love Lucy, The Red Skelton Show, The Jackie Gleason Show* and *The Jack Benny Program*. As a joke teller, Dad revelled in an epoch of predictable punchlines.

"Heard it all a thousand times, Corky," deadpanned Mum, sipping her tea.

Dad got Tuesday respite when I began to take Mum to an adult daycare. After ten years of worsening dementia, Mum suffered a fall and a broken hip, and she went from home to hospital to nursing home. A bacterial infection took her in the end. Dad lasted another year, until a series of falls and pneumonia took him as well.

Those visits with Mum and Dad developed the patience, tolerance and understanding I would need with Steve—like training wheels.

//

Steve and I have spent more than half our lifetimes away from home and each other—time to forge our own paths. Except that he has a chronic mental illness. He has fallen into an abyss. Still. I sense that there might be more to his life than the cave of delusion Plato spoke of.[17]

Plato, a classical Greek philosopher, told a story of three men chained together in a cave. They faced a blank wall on which shadows of passersby were cast from a fire that burned behind them. The shadow world was their only reality, until one of the prisoners broke free of his bonds and ventured out into the blinding world of reality.

The bonds of mental illness are about to loosen for Steve: to see beyond the shadows (and echoes and voices). He doesn't tell me why he comes on weekly outings with me.

Was it boredom? Was it curiosity? Was it desperation?

This HSP imagines how it might have come to be.

///

"Don't you look dapper," says Bart later that winter afternoon, after Dad's memorial.

"Shut up, we've got work to do," says Steve, emptying his largest carryall cart.

"Are we leaving the hobbit hole for a while?" asks Bilbo.

"An hour should do," says Steve.

"I'm scared of the dark," says Bart.

"People play tricks in the dark," says Clown.

"Are you dipsticks coming or not?" Steve knows that they are.

He takes off the memorial suit and rolls up the shirt, pants, jacket and tie in the plastic covering. He pulls on layers of dingy clothing, leaving the suit on the bed. He lifts the cart over the narrow slip of sidewalk along the side of the house, and out into the back lane.

Three blocks east they find what they are looking for—a dumpster, with discarded bicycle wheels and frames jutting out, skeletal bones in the late afternoon light. It is a large bin near a second-hand bicycle shop. Steve looks in with the assist of two small flashlights wedged between his fingers.

"Good stuff," says Steve.

"There are trolls in this laneway...you may need the ring," says Bilbo.

All Steve hears is the *clang* of a metal piece, dropping to the bottom of the dumpster.

Half a laneway away, two ne'er-do-wells spray graffiti obscenities and racial slurs on garage doors and any other flat surface. They spy Steve, braced on the lip of the dumpster. The dumpster blocks Steve's view of them, but they are on the lookout for mischief.

"Tip him in," one mouths and gestures to the other.

"Yeah," the other punk mouths back with a thumbs-up.

They creep up behind Steve and catapult him into the dumpster.

"Heave ho," cries one.

"Bombs away," chimes the other.

Steve tips easily, since he is leaning precariously over the edge. The bicycle parts break his fall. His leather jacket, thick wool toque, heavy work pants and natural burliness buffer him. The flashlights shine up from the dark bottom, temporarily blinding him, his glasses askew.

Steve hears spray cans hissing, along with voices: "Retard. Bastard. Die."

The bad boys repeat the chant, laughing in spasms, while they spray and thud the canisters against the metal exterior.

RETARD

BASTARD

DIE

Steve scrambles on the uneven surface and retrieves his mini-flashlights. He ejects bicycle parts with his free hand in hopes of scaring them off. He steadies himself against one side of the bin as they return the volley. From the outside, bicycle parts are flying. From the inside, it is as terrifying and immobilizing as the clatter of falling rocks at the base of a cliff.

"Find something better to do, you sons of bitches," says a neighbour across the laneway, who opens his back gate, letting out two guard dogs.

"I hope your sorry asses sting," yells the dogs' owner.

The punks take off, dogs growling and nipping at them.

The stress and noise bring on a hallucination for Steve—a simple visual one of shadow and light. It scrolls across the dumpster's interior like a prelude to a Hitchcock movie. It takes geometric form and morphs into a more complex hallucination with lifelike images, a scene unfolding. He sees and hears orc-like monsters.

Orcs are part human, part goblin, with fangs for foraging and green-tinged skin. Slathering silhouettes—they are Steve's worst nightmare, the worst of what his hallucinations can bring.

Tolkien borrowed orcs from Norse folk tales. Pop culture continues to use them as bad guys in video games. They are our inner monsters. Steve hears a whistle (the dog owner reels in his dogs).

The short film reels uncontrollably to an end. He spies a pop can tab at the bottom of the bin and retrieves it.

"Bilbo's ring," he says as he slips it on. His heart is thumping. With the ring on his pinky, he feels empowered.

"Orc a Cork; orc a Cork; orc a Cork," Steve mumbles, until he has a better idea. "Cork an orc; Cork an orc; Cork an orc." A reverse mantra puts a stopper in it.

All goes quiet. He creates a ladder with bike frames against the inside of the dumpster and hoists himself up and out. The dogs snarl from inside the fence. The vigilante neighbour has called them back and slammed his door, unaware of Steve in the dumpster. Clown mimes innocence. Bart sobs. Bilbo pats Bart's shoulder. They line the edge of the dumpster.

"I warned you. Trolls," says Bilbo.

"Speak up next time, you useless turd," says Steve. He flicks Bilbo's ring off his pinky.

Bilbo catches it and slips it in Steve's pocket. "Please, you keep it," says Bilbo.

Steve examines the graffiti-style scrawl on the dumpster. He reads the hateful words and then picks up the black and white spray cans that the punks dropped in their hasty escape.

"I am," Steve says to Bilbo.

Steve sprays black as a letter blotter. "Hsssst."

"Yes, you are," smiles Bilbo.

Steve's voice is no longer swallowed in fear. It is resonant. He waits for the black to dry.

He blots out the RET of "retard" and the BAST of "bastard" with dark paint. He blots out the two Ds:

RETARD becomes *AR*.

BASTARD becomes *AR*.

"Hsssst."

He blots out more syllables and reworks the lettering with white spray paint. The new words roll off his tongue like effervescence. It is scripted. It is final.

He blots the D of "die," and all that's left is IE—i.e., Latin for "that is to say."

RETARD becomes *AR*   *I AM ARTIST*

BASTARD becomes *AR*   *ARTIST*

DIE becomes *IE*   *IE I AM*

"I know you are, but what am I?" says Clown.

Steve throws the cans into the dumpster and spotlights his work with the flashlights, humming the *Bugs Bunny* theme song.

"That's all folks," says Steve.

Steve's spray paint and flashing lights stream through his hapless helpers. They giggle. Bart does flips. Bilbo balances. Clown clowns along the ledge in the spotlights. Steve props two bike wheels from the laneway litter onto his buggy and rolls the cart home in the dusk.

%

That's what I think happened...or something like it. He never tells me whether he was fed up with the shadows, the hallucinations—with the cave of his hoarded existence.

"Steve, why did you come with me on Tuesdays?" I want to ask. "What gave you the courage?"

%

Bonnie and I are lesson planning. We are teaching partners. She hovers over our shared desk with a mind map—its central circle and six adjoining circles. We team teach the first day of every semester with our adult immigrant students who have the basics of English. We introduce ourselves to them, and then we model how to interview each other using open-ended phrases like "Tell me about your...(family, hobbies, education, work, travels, dreams)."

We model the interview on whiteboards (she at the front and me at the side) with two templates of six circles: one for Bonnie, one for me. She stands at one with my name in the middle; I stand at the other, her name in the middle.

"Here's the introduction. They work in pairs," I say to Bonnie.

"Pair up with a student from a different country," she says.

"To ensure they speak English," I add.

"We've got the *Family* and *Hobby* circles covered...you: mother, daughter, wife, tennis player, hiker. Us: walkers, book clubbers. Me: wife, sister, skier, swimmer, kayaker, singer, yogi, cyclist, poet."

We refer to our notes. "That list makes me look lame," says Bonnie.

"What do you mean?" I say. "You're the awesome Mother."

"You're the Entertainer," says Bonnie.

Bonnie is an organizer who finds things, files things and brings things together in a way I can't. "Add in where you're from, where you've been—travel plans," she says.

"What else?" I say.

"Dreams," she says.

"What we plan to do?"

"I want to be a grandmother. How about you?"

"Without procreation, creation will have to do."

"You've published poetry. You're a writer."

"Okay, I am."

"Come on, say it," says Bonnie.

"I am a writer." I do more than hedge. I allege.

%

"Hey, Darren." (We're on the phone.)

"Let's meet up with Steve and go over the trust," says Darren. Darren and I plan to review the trusteeship over coffee with Steve, and then drop him back home.

"I'm on my way. See you in half an hour. Let's take one car to Steve's," I suggest.

"What's *she* doing here?" asks Steve, as I follow Darren up the front steps.

"Joan and I are your trustees, Steve, handling Mum and Dad's gift to you," says Darren.

"You sound like captors. A pair of pirates," says Steve.

"You can afford a new bicycle or computer. Let Joan know. How's the bank account?" asks Darren.

"Okay. Here's the suit." Steve passes the rolled-up bag to Darren. "Thanks."

"Steve, how 'bout I swing by on Tuesdays?" I ask.

"What? Are you going to babysit Steve?" whispers Darren, out of Steve's hearing.

"We'll find out what programs Coastal Health offers," I say.

"Okay," says Steve.

※

Steve and I sign in at the Coast Mental Health Clubhouse and register for a computer session. Each week we go, Steve forgets how to sign in, and he forgets his password. He doesn't type. The programs offered are vocational: godsends for many, but not for Steve. Their programs remind him of jobs he's done and lost over the years. One good thing about our age gap and estrangement overall is that I don't remind him of his wife (I hadn't met her), his three sons (one son born in Steve's twenties to a girlfriend who'd raised the child in another town, and two sons, born in his thirties, with whom he'd spent a few of their toddler years) or his friends and associates. Untreated mental illness soured relationships. All lost. He tastes acrid disappointment.

"This here's a deadbeat dad," he's told me before.

Some weeks he wears an orange reflective bib like a road worker. One week they can't find his name on the membership roster, which consists mostly of vocational clientele. Steve is standing out, in neon.

"I'm not a member here. Register yourself, Joan. *You're* the email queen."

"Okay Steve. We'll find something else, somewhere else," I say over the dollar-a-plate lunch.

I become the weekly emailer in communiqués to his three sons and to our siblings. I share our Tuesdays with them. An email correspondence is established. The two Hawaiian-American brothers and the Canadian half-brother make contact with one another on social media. They then plan to meet up. Steve is uniting us—grouting our tiles in place.

I go to a "Working Together to Educate Families" conference to learn about paranoid schizophrenia: the diagnosis that Steve never acknowledges. This lack of awareness is called anosognosia or lack of insight, according to the National Alliance on Mental Illness (NAMI).[18]

He may have mentioned having schizophrenia twice...alluding to how the family has branded him.

"There are physical and biochemical changes in the brain with this illness," says the speaker.

※

Steve would return home in his early twenties for the occasional Sunday dinner, where he would talk hippie-talk: about the bourgeoisie (the family) versus the proletariat (him). We were a brief testing ground for Marxist theories about the exploitive middle class (us) and the propertyless worker (him). As a young teenager, I had no idea how far his *Mad Mag/Simpsons/Saturday Night Live* philosophy had moved toward counterculture.

"That's bullshit," Dad would say, leaving the table. End of conversation, after which Steve's visits came less often.

The hippie movement masked the physical and biochemical changes taking place as his illness progressed. At weddings, Steve arrived in sandals with leather-ringed big toes, an open-necked shirt, buttonless, with multicoloured embroidery, and raggedy jeans, emanating incense. Cool. Steve's posturing and funny voices? Not cool. Nobody got his jokes but him. He was unperturbed yet...disturbed.

※

Symposium speaker: "Schizophrenia is not a split personality or any result or personal failure of the individual or parent."

Mum and Dad had had those conversations. "Maybe it's in your family, not mine," said Mum.

"What about your twin sister?" asked Dad.

"What are we going to do today, Gertie?" Mum remembered her sister's dependency. Her sister had gone with her to boarding school. They were eleven years of age. Their mother, my grandmother, still had a toddler at home. Becoming a dependent twin's keeper felt like too much responsibility for Mum.

When the Second World War broke out, Aunt Kay signed up for the British Army. Mum signed up for the Royal Air Force. She liked the blue uniform that her sister was not wearing. Mum became a coder and decipherer with a puzzler's mind. A commanding officer recruited her after noticing the complex knitting patterns and crossword puzzles she was doing.

Mum and her sister's differences didn't add up to mental illness. One was as musically gifted in piano as the other (Mum) was in singing. Mum won the 1934 Welsh Eisteddfod Soprano Solo competition: one of her proudest moments.

None of our immediate aunts and uncles displayed signs of mental illness, at least none I knew of. Two of Mum's siblings became doctors; two became lawyers. Dad's brothers worked in business, and all the men were WW II veterans. Dad's sisters married veterans and raised families in the fifties and sixties.

Later, hints of depressive illness or mood disorders bubble up on both sides. Nonetheless, schizophrenia as a primary psychotic illness is missing from all these histories. Who to blame?

※

The blame game. And that expression Steve keeps repeating: "No praise, no blame." Surely praise is a good thing? It is addictive. But blame? Blame's another game altogether.

At the mental health symposium, I sit next to two friendly psychiatric nurses. The speaker resumes the discourse: "Age of onset is in the prime: between sixteen and twenty-five...more common than most people think...one in a hundred people, or one in seven if it's in the family," the symposium speaker says.

I think about what is being said, in my lateral-thinking way: *We are seven. Seven is how birds flock. Not in massive swarms like starlings, but in subgroups within those swarms. Float like a fish or fly like a bird. Think 3-D with room to get away. Fortify the flanks. Two and two and two and you. I've got your back. Bird. Fish. Friend.*

Seven signifies completeness: the seven-day creation story, the seven continents, the seven seas, the seven colours of the rainbow and the seven notes of the scale. Lucky seven in dice. As one of seven children, I use my lateral logic to warrant helping Steve. My singing group might've just sung "If Just One Person Believes in You."[19] I am the one. The one he can count on. Is that why he's given me an abacus?

"Hang it here, on the rear-view mirror, Joan," says Steve from the passenger side in my vehicle.

"As long as it doesn't block my vision," I say.

I hear Dad's insurance agent voice: "Don't have anything dangling from your rear-view mirror."

Light, colourful and on many occasions helpful in finding the car in a busy parking lot, it doesn't block my vision. And neither does Steve.

※

"Strange posturing, bizarre behaviour, agitation, inappropriate laughter, deteriorating personal hygiene, social withdrawal, unusual beliefs, loss of motivation," says the symposium speaker in describing schizophrenia symptoms.

"Check, check, check...and check," I'm thinking.

An announcement comes on for a change in the next session—Peer Counselling. It is not the one I planned on attending. "Wait, not that one," I say aloud to the two nurses. By now, I've shared a bit of history with them. "Steve doesn't want a peer. I already asked him about that," I say.

"Meet up with someone who shares *your* disability, Joan," he's told me.

"This seminar will be good for you," say the nurses.

※

From the same womb, I am familiar and familial. I listen; I provide friendship and caring. Darren takes care of Steve's housing, taxes, health and governmental glitches. I am the enthusiast—from the Greek *en theo*, with God. Steve's peer pal.

"Couldn't it be better?" I wonder who else might join Steve's team. What if he had a peer who understood the illness? Who had the illness? What if he had a tennis-playing peer? Tennis is a high-impact, stop-start game that my artificial hips don't easily tolerate—a game that I never learned to play very well. While I am considering a team approach, Steve isn't.

In terms of involvement with people, Steve is a minimalist. He has a one-on-one relationship with his psychiatrist, Dr. P, who has told me, "I never believed Steve would stick with monthly visits for this long." Theirs is a psychiatrist-patient relationship (a bit one-sided no matter how good a listener the other is). Those meetings, which I sometimes attend, are conversations about life in general. Transpiring for twenty years, they culminate with prescription needs.

"We never put Steve on antipsychotics," Dr. P tells me at one of those appointments. Up until the 1980s, the downside of antipsychotics came with side effects such as muscle stiffness, tremors and abnormal movements that would, the drug companies suggested, worsen over time.[20] Steve doesn't tell me what medications he's tried. What worked? What didn't? "He has loose associations, also known as a type of mania or thought disorder," says Dr. P.

In some circles, that is termed "creative thinking." Dr. Edward de Bono, a physician and psychologist, coined the term "lateral thinking." In other circles, it's called "knight's move thinking." The chess game pieces (the knights) move forward, then sideways. Logical liaisons are lacking. Connections happen instead, in rhymes, sounds and free associations.

Steve Jobs valued lateral thinking highly. So do NASA, Honda, Harvard and my bro. So do I. Steve's loose associations, however, are hard for me to track.

"If you wait long enough, Steve always makes his point," Dr. P says.

Most people don't wait. The seconds tick away. People get ticked off.

Steve has never locked in to an automatic response. Never a pat answer. On Tuesdays, I give him the time it takes.

Steve shuns social workers and therapists. One-on-one is his favourite interaction. One-on-one is therapeutic. Any more than that creates imbalance: triggers for paranoia. Paranoia comes from the Greek word for "madness." For those with paranoid schizophrenia, delusional beliefs accompany the split in the thinking process. Delusions, disorganized speech and behaviour are positive symptoms, so termed because they are in excess of the norm. The negative symptoms are a loss of normal functioning: flat emotions, a lack of motivation and concentration. Positive symptoms have nothing to do with positivity or confidence. Negative symptoms are unrelated to a lack of confidence. This negativity equates with deficit; the positivity equates with excess. They are like puzzle pieces. Puzzling to me in that what the experts say doesn't always fit into the Steve Puzzle.

Sometimes I feel, Why me? Without shirking my new duty, I feel ill-prepared to deal with such a complicated illness: such a complicated brother. Teaching teenagers has taught me to take my fair share of kidding and testing of boundaries. Steve tests me. My inner voice argues, "Maybe there is a part of you that is able to take on this new role."

And maybe it isn't as new as I think.

%

The two psychiatric nurses each take one of my elbows. They've been my guardian angels this day. I tuck in, under their widespread wings.

Peer counselling? Peers are equals. A jury is made up of peers. It's not up to me to judge.

The Canadian Mental Health Association (CMHA) provides Peer Support Worker certification. Steve could have that tennis-playing peer—someone who suffers from schizophrenia, someone who understands. In addition to Peer Supporters, CMHA also trains Peer Support Mentors and Family Peer Supporters. Steve says no to the former and yes to the latter. That is to say, he hasn't turned me down.

Steve and I are from the same flock, the same school of fish. Same mother stream. Root, roost. Nest of understanding. In that sense, we are peer siblings.

The National Alliance on Mental Illness (NAMI) has communication guidelines on its website[21] that advise reflective listening focused solely on understanding, not reacting to, the afflicted one.

Back at the conference, I jot down a list:

Use short, clear sentences (like I do for my adult ESL students).

Avoid distractions. (Keep the car radio off.)

Sit quietly and wait (for Steve to initiate the conversation).

Be pleasant. Be firm. Listen. (Don't take off on my own lateral-thinking tangents.)

Give (Steve) *time and space to respond.*

Be empathetic and uncritical.

Set limits. (No F-bombs, Steve!)

Use eye contact. (Even if he doesn't.)

Breathe.

Back home, I leaf through the materials I've picked up this day. There is a handout making mention of a program called the Art Studios.[22] It is described as a safe, respectful and accepting community where people with a major mental illness diagnosis can thrive, in co-operation with rehabilitation staff. The word *thrive*, in this context, thrills me.

I call. Darren, Steve and I go to an Art Studios orientation. It is accessible from Steve's home, on his bus route. For me it is a broader arc east, but it is a far better fit. I meet him there.

Ann Webborn is an Art Studios occupational therapist and artist who speaks to Steve directly. She is a communicator. She follows the guidelines I've been studying to the tee. He listens to her. A connection is made. After a session at the Art Studios, Steve and I are about to grab a snack, when I see a friend from Nordic skiing circles walking toward us.

I tell myself, *Don't shy away. Don't be embarrassed to introduce your brother.*

"Hi, Robert, how's it going? Steve, this is Robert."

"Hi," Steve says.

"Just on a late lunch break...what are you doing over here?" Robert knows Ken and I are North Vancouverites.

"My brother and I are doing art. This is my brother, Steve."

"What kind of art do you do?" Robert turns to Steve. Steve has no reply.

///

Conté crayons are square-edged sticks of compressed charcoal or graphite in a range of colours, from sanguine to brown, black, grey and white. Conté crayons bind together with a wax or clay base. Steve and I are finding a bond, but at times it feels more like a bind.

Conte is French for an imaginative story or tale. Steve's the raconteur. I'm the re-counter: the witness he can relate to and count on (thus the abacus). For Steve, it is no counting game. Fingertip-shaped bruises appear on my upper arm—Steve's way of separating me from illusion. Me, a reality. Him, starting to dabble in it.

///

Creation-Conjugation
I am, I'm, I'm not, am I? Yes, I am. No, I'm not. Uh uh.
He is, he's, he's not, is he? Yes, he is. No, he's not. He isn't.
She is, she's, she's not, is she? Yes, she is. No, she's not. She isn't.
We are, we're, we're not, are we? Yes, we are. No, we're not. We aren't.
Who we are.

///

Creation myths exist across religious traditions. Mythic figures transform from human to animal and back again. Might Steve be able to transform mental illness into something more productive, creative and positive? His phoenix is awakening, stirring from the ashes. He scoops a piece of charcoal from the ashen debris, and puts it in his pocket in a determination to don a new role beyond that of his diagnosis.

CHAPTER 3

Transfer, Stencil and Collage

I HAVE SIX DAYS to recover from one day with Steve. The Art Studios sessions are new for me. So is spending talk-time with Steve afterwards, doing errands and having lunch. The après-art time allows for communication, but talking isn't easy for or with my brother. We're both working hard to reach the other.

The rest of the week, I'm with Ken or friends. I am alone in short patches. I prepare my ESL students to communicate in their new culture. Maybe Steve is also learning to communicate again. When not at work or home, I Nordic ski, bicycle or kayak tour. I sing with a vocal ensemble and do yoga, swim indoors or outdoors, year-round.

When my adult ESL students ask whether I have children, my response is, "No, I have hobbies."

※

It's Tuesday morning. I lie in bed, listening to a CBC radio newscast, wondering if a wrongdoer in the news report could be Steve. Arsonist, murderer, robber? Is he the victim, or the perpetrator?

That I envisage this brother of mine capable of such things is the extent of my fear-mongering.

"In local news, a man was seen running away after an attempted break-in..."

"A man in his fifties is being sought in an assault on the East Side..."

"One man is dead in a hit and run on Main Street..."

"A bus driver is injured and the police are looking for witnesses..."

"A fire at a hoarder's suite claims one life..."

I take a deep breath, get in the car and head over town, reminding myself, "I'm here to help him (or to help Ann, the occupational therapist and artist leading his sketch group) focus on instructions, rechannel distractions and calm anxiety."

Knowing he's been isolated, I want to give him space and, at the same time, be a calming presence. I know he's out of practice with having a peer or making social interaction with anyone other than bank tellers or cashiers. I am an ear for what's in his head.

Steve's language gets ribald at times, and this sets him off. "Steve, please don't use the F-bomb." And he doesn't.

One day out of seven, we come together like the seven colours of the prism. We harmonize. We clash. The odd time, we blend. "I'm one of seven," I say to myself. "Seven days in a week: I can give him one day."

We are there. The Art Studios is a government-funded Vancouver Coastal Health facility. The Vancouver Recovery Through Art Society, with help from its friends the VGH and UBC Hospital Foundation and others, supports the Art Studios initiatives. The Art Studios is committed to providing art classes and studio space, and to fostering mental health and addictions recovery and growth through art.

Our class starts with introductions. Ten students sit around a table in a brightly lit studio space, cupboards filled with bountiful art supplies. Ann Webborn facilitates the icebreaker. Nowadays, students train to become facilitators. They blossom under a therapeutic heat lamp. That's the power of art.

"Hi, I'm Sandy. I'm not really an artist. I used to do art but haven't for ages."

"Hi, I'm Joe. My art has been mostly doodles."

"My name is Beth. I've never called myself an artist, but…"

Each student says more or less the same thing. They are shy about their art. Ann gives Steve time to respond. When it's his turn, he says, "I'm Steve. My problem is my mouth."

This admission astounds me. He isn't unsure of his artistic ability. He's more worried about what might slip out of his mouth, Tourette's-like.

After class, we meet up with Darren for coffee. Steve grimaces when I mention his *mouth* comment, as if that is my problem. For big-brother Darren, problem solving is direct. His direct approach works well with Steve.

"Just shut up and draw," Darren says. Succinct. And, for the most part, Steve does just that.

Classes unfold at the Art Studios.

If Steve rides his bike, I load it in the car afterwards and we go to the Safeway at Oakridge Centre for groceries. If he takes the bus, we pack his buggy and bags in the back of the car. Most Tuesdays we have lunch in the food court. Sometimes we go to a restaurant, but the food court is less formal. There, speaking loudly is necessary over the din. Steve always speaks loudly over his inner din. In a restaurant, I pick a booth and hope for a tolerant waiter.

Shopping at Safeway, I follow Steve's instructions: "Get two two-litre jugs of 2 percent milk, Joan."

"That's a lot of milk, Steve. Won't it go bad?"

"I have to drink more. It's my medication."

"Okay…meet you at the till."

"Oh, and get some yogurt, if it's on sale."

I run a tab on my credit card, save the receipts and write myself a check every couple of months. That is my job as trustee. I make dietary suggestions like less soda pop, less meat, less coffee. Gently.

The fruit and vegetables Steve chooses come from Kin's Market dollar bin. We go there after shopping at Safeway and lunch in the food court, on the way back to the car.

Steve adds bread and cheese to his list, or he asks me if I've ever tried kiwi fruit, or how I cook spaghetti. We get a hamburger and fries at A&W. He likes burger specials, so he brings the coupons that come through his mailbox. He gets a Mama, Papa or Teen Burger and a tall Coke. I have the Veggie Burger.

My husband and I have been vegetarians who eat fish and dairy, called pescatarians, ever since Ken's recovery from colon cancer. After studying nutrition and diet, we came to a regime that works for us: plant-based and a bit dull to most palates. We eat little spiced or processed food. But this is my day out with Steve. I allow myself a bit of junk food.

Steve's always been a Coca-Cola guy. When we were kids, it came in glass bottles that he savoured like a connoisseur. If I happened to be downstairs watching the same TV show as him, he might have offered me a juice-glass-full from his sixteen-ounce glass bottle. The 1960s Coca-Cola jingle suggested that "fun" and "fizzy" were friends. I'd propose a toast but Steve's toast is lukewarm.

Our first food-court lunch, I get two cups and start to pour.

"I can pour my own," he says.

"Steve, pouring for the other person is just something friends do."

Before long, he is pouring. We split the fries. New York Fries or the ones from Safeway's deli: we compare texture and taste. Too skinny, too fat, too salty, too crispy. When it is my turn, I get a falafel, or tacos, or a side salad.

"Cover Joan's gas money," Darren tells Steve. How he calculates how much that is, I never work out, but what he gives me is uncannily accurate. "Try a thank you every so often," Darren adds. "It won't kill you."

Steve's thank yous are a bit forced at first. Soon, it's a habit for which I am grateful. I stop wondering what to say. He pours out more than Coke. He pours out what he's been thinking about all week.

"Joan, do you have old-timers?" he says when I slip up.

His doctor may have referenced schizophrenia-related disorders like working-memory loss. Steve's memory is probably better than an elephant's (those noble creatures who find fifty-year survival stores of food and water). Steve's memory roots back to all the people he's ever known.

Reminding me of what I've forgotten does make me a bit crabby.

"Joan, your mood disorder is acting up again."

He likes these asides. I let them go. I don't even know what a mood disorder is. Turns out, Steve's lithium medication is a mood stabilizer.

"The Cochrane Collaboration, known for their high-quality reviews and meta-analyses, published a systematic review of the efficacy of lithium as used to treat schizophrenia."[23]

Twenty-two studies and 763 participants later, the 2015 study concluded, "One can imagine that a clinician, having exhausted all other treatment options, may see the appeal of a non-specific drug with a broad 'dampening' effect on neurotransmitter function."[24]

I don't know what treatment options were tried on Steve. Neither do I question the relationship between Steve and Dr. P, which seems to be a good one.

Steve has a potpourri of schizophrenia's negative symptoms, such as apathy and a flattened emotional effect. Nevertheless, he never misses one of our meetups. He can muster motivation for our one day a week.

I dream a Steve rant. His real-time rants are in the third person. Words like "you" or "I" are left out. The third person isn't him. It's a metaphor of him: "The argument is, Joan, take a pigeon and pen it up (put it in a sack)—all cooing and cajoling on its perch—pooing and pecking—scoop it up in a bag and throw it into a dungeon—blast the burlap sack through with shotgun pellets—then pull pidgey out: bloodied, feathers flying. Ask it to fly—no, don't ask; demand that it fly: 'Fly, you little bastard.'"

"Okay Steve. Watch your language," my dream self says, much as my real self does. (If I remain calm, maybe he will.)

"And just to show the dungeon keeper what he's made of, pidgey flops over to the garret window and looks down—no other pidgeys around, no pooing, pecking, cooing or cajoling—and pronounces, 'Okay, you son of a bitch, watch me fly.' One-winged, with blood spraying all around, a rainbow forming from the red-orange-yellow, he dives head first into a pot of gold; a cooing rhapsody, till the crash."

I never know how to respond to these rants. Unfathomable fragments. This one is rational compared to the ones he gives in real life. Representationally, it's the best I can do.

※

I meet Steve again at the Art Studios a week later. I am a fear allayer, of both his and mine.

Does he have friends? What does he do all week?

I don't go inside his place. He doesn't invite me. I carry half of his shopping bags and art paraphernalia to the top step.

He's showing me his weekly haunts: Value Village, the Salvation Army and St. Vincent's Thrift Store, plus a few food stops. He is letting me in to his life.

※

If Steve starts a rant with Ann in an art session, she says, "Let's not talk right now, Steve." Or, "Steve, come back to that later. We'll talk about it at the break."

In a second silkscreening session, the homework is a design for a tee-shirt, but Steve hasn't done it. Other students pull out designs they've drawn. He fiddles with a plastic toy that he pulls from his pocket. I feel discouraged at his lack of interest, or apparent lack of interest.

"Photocopy this, Joan."

"Photocopy a 3-D toy? It's a 2-D copier."

"Just do it, Joan. You're my manager."

Although a bit lumpy under the lid, it works. From that image, he draws a Vintage Sewer Spiker variation from the 1984 comic book *Teenage Mutant Ninja Turtles*,[25] one he didn't get a chance to read to his two young sons, but a series he knows by heart (and perhaps knows that they'll remember). But this isn't his plan.

"Is that going to be your tee-shirt design, Steve?"

"No." He's looking at the image. He flips the page and starts again.

Steve launches into a variation of Serendipity the Pink Dragon. Without children of my own, I'm not up to date on kid lit or TV programming. Apparently, Serendipity is a wyvern or winged baby dragon from a popular 1980s anime TV series. Steve's rendition of this "dragonette" is much less fearsome than an armoured Ninja. She's a cute adaptation, and she is his choice for the design. Steve's artistic sprout is about to take wing. He produces her in a minute or two. She's going to soften up all the men in our family (if they dare to wear her).

American art teacher and author Betty Edwards describes imagination as a perceptual skill, a dialogue in achieving art with a capital A.[26] It's as if she's been looking over Steve's shoulder at the Art Studios:

"The artist has a vague idea, let's say, to draw a creature...perhaps a winged dragon. The artist...begins to draw, making a few marks that perhaps indicate the head of the dragon. Those marks trigger an imagined extension and elaboration...the artist 'sees' or envisions... then draws in the imagined extension with new marks. That triggers an expanded image, perhaps the body and wings, now 'seen.'...This dialogue continues until the artwork is finished."[27]

Nick Bantock, author of the *Griffin and Sabine* trilogy, is one of Steve's preferred artist authors. His book *The Artful Dodger* is an autobiographical amalgam of his multi-facets: book cover illustrator, quirky pop-up creator and storyteller. Bantock sees all winged creatures as transitional.[28] Ancient cultures saw winged creatures soaring toward higher knowledge and freedom.

Whatever Steve's sweet dragonette represents, what he produces fills me with awe. On my own, driving home in the car, I want to shout, "Steve's artistic soul is alive!" or "Steve's still got it!" or "Steve's illness hasn't undermined his talent!" or all of the above, separately, in intermittent outbursts. In the moment when he's drawing her, I'm speechless.

We've been panning, sifting and digging for several months, looking for some meaningful purpose, and a nugget has just surfaced—a bit tarnished, but pure gold.

///

Was it fate that in 1983, when *Serendipity the Pink Dragon* aired as a hand-drawn Japanese animation or anime (which became a TV series), Steve's wife had left three winters earlier, taking their three- and four-year-old sons with her, with an idea to return in the spring? The pink dragon egg hatched, but the reunion didn't.

He sent the boys care packages instead that were "heady mixtures of various readings, pictures, curiosities, useful and useless, rare and mundane items. Very often he'd send something exactly right for the boys' interests at that time," his wife tells me later.

He's maintained a fascination with children's toys—and children's cartoon images like the baby dragon. So what if his "boys" are thirtyish by the time they receive their tee-shirts? By the time we do the mail-out, Steve has a grandson. Time warps when one is alone and troubled. To Steve, toddlers are a delight—curious and energetic, but, most of all, non-judgmental.

///

Steve's landlord doesn't have cable for TV running into the house. I pick up some second-hand DVDs and a player for Steve.

He doesn't need cable to watch DVDs. He, the artist-animator, enjoys the playfulness of cartoons, much as he enjoyed them in his short term as a father.

※

My serendipity or good fortune unfolded with Ken's and my wedding in December 1983. Steve wasn't well enough to attend. That's what I tell myself. (I didn't want his presence marring my big day.) In the spring of 1984 Ken and I moved into a townhouse in Kitsilano, not far from Steve's old neighbourhood.

The neighbourhood's 1967 hippie glory days (that was the year he moved away from home) were long gone, but Fourth Avenue kept calling him back. There he was—a few blocks from my new home, grocery shopping at Safeway. Or was he just drifting through, gaunt and filthy? I recognized something about the way he carried himself: upright like a gymnast.

"Hi Steve," I said, and he uttered some kind of recognition. He knew me. "Do you want to go for coffee?" I asked.

We crossed the street to an outdoor café. We sat. For three hours, I listened to him rant. After we parted, I went home and cried. More than lost, he was ill. I called Darren, who put in place the accommodation with Lawrence and the psychiatric care with Dr. P.

I didn't imagine that I had anything to offer him at that time except pity. Pity put me above Steve. I was better off, wasn't I? Pity wasn't anything he needed or deserved, but I had to experience my own pain and loss: Ken's and my infertility, my hip replacements, Ken's colon cancer, the eldercare and passing of Mum and Dad. It took twenty years before Steve and I began meetups. Time is a great leveller.

That brings us up to date. I've gone beyond pity to sympathize with his situation, but Steve wants more. He wants my share in the quest. He's going to use his middle-child power of negotiation to make that happen. I just don't know it yet.

※

Steve transfers the stencil of his baby dragon adaptation onto a polyester screen. We're at an Art Studios session. He stretches and staples it onto the frame. I've bought the supplies: water-based paint, a squeegee and blank white tee-shirts, as per the instruction list. We do a couple of testers in the third and final class.

I set up a workshop workbench at my place. Thanksgiving produces a run of shirts for Christmas presents. Twenty of them, for anyone I can think of who might wear a baby dragon tee. My sister, Sally, picks Steve up and drives him over, and we three become a printing-press gang—silkscreening from the garage.

The squeegee drags across the screen and fills the open-mesh apertures with ink. A reverse stroke squishes through the mesh onto the tee-shirt, imposing the design and blanking out what is impermeable. In this transfer process, Steve is transforming along with the art that is oozing out of his pores. He is temporarily blanking out an illness that has been, up until now, impervious to change.

Steve is fully engrossed, mixing red, yellow, blue, black, white and brass fabric paint, heedless of the one-paint-colour-at-a-time suggested method.

Hungarian psychologist Mihaly Csikszentmihalyi refers to flow as the root of happiness.[29] When one is completely engaged in the groove or zone, there's no attention left for ego, apathy or boredom. We take control and focus in a clear, serene and timeless way called ecstasy. Ecstasy, from the Greek, means being outside body or mind—putting ourselves aside. For Steve, putting himself aside is restful. This is where he wants to be.

We wash and dry the frame between applications. Once squeegeed, a hot dryer sets the image.

We adjourn upstairs for stuffed squash and wild rice—dessert after artistic indulgence.

※

Screen printing is just one form of stencilling. Prehistoric cave artists blew pigment through hollowed-out bones onto splayed left hands (their stencils). The method became popularized some eighteen thousand years later, with 1960s pop artist Andy Warhol projecting silk-screen images of Marilyn Monroe, Jackie Onassis and Elvis Presley. Steve knew of Warhol's emergence as a visual artist: an artist twenty years his senior who exhibited from the 1960s to the 1980s in multimedia, notably *100 Soup Cans, 100 Coke Bottles, 100 Dollar Bills.*

Steve studied the pioneers of the Cubist movement, Picasso and Braque, in his time at the Vancouver School of Art (the forerunner of Emily Carr University of Art and Design). Picasso and Braque pushed the art form of stencilling into collage. Gluing on parts to make a new whole stretched their painterly style into the realms of sculpture, raising the surface, giving it nap.

Another contemporary of Picasso, Henri Matisse, who was chair- and bed-bound after abdominal surgery, created paper-cut collage (what Matisse termed "painting with scissors") for wall hangings, scarf patterns, tapestries, rugs and stained-glass windows.

Steve likes drawing; he leaves the cutting and transferring of images to me, aside from some early stencilling at the Art Studios with Ann. He lends me his decorative pinking shears for the task.

I accept his invitation to collage. Collage is all about attachment. He's given me the parts. The composition is multimedia: poetry, prose and art. Glued together to create a new whole: his influence— stuck on me.

CHAPTER 4

Charcoal

ANN WEBBORN IS FACILITATING a final sketch session at the Art Studios and asks the class to copy an image. The details read: "Colorplate 57, *The Moroccans*. 1916. Canvas. 71-3/8 x 110 inches (181.3 x 279.4 cm). Collection, The Museum of Modern Art, New York. Gift of Mr. and Mrs. Samuel A. Marx."

The still life contains a jumble of circular shapes. Steve copies them in thirty minutes. The charcoal waltzes under his grip. What's exciting about the composition is that Steve seems to recognize the language it speaks. The language of art is elemental; it has seven elements—line, shape, space, value, texture, colour and form. Here's a language that doesn't confuse. Nor does it distract or sideline him in any way. Ann has referred to each element throughout the ten-week class. I've been there as an observer, and today's exercise is a culmination of these components.

Steve uses a mixture of horizontal, vertical, diagonal and curved *lines* in a variety of widths. The composition comprises geometric (rectangles, circles, squares) *shapes* enclosed in *lines* that define height and width. Around the *shapes* are unoccupied *spaces* that give a feeling of depth or gravity in the Moroccan heat of contrasts. Steve's dark to light *values* range from charcoal shading to a Conté crayon's pale reddish hue. The simulated illusion of *texture* is in the rind of market melons and gourds.

Line, shape, space, value and texture are the five elements expressed in this composition (most artworks encompass at least two elements). *Form* refers more to sculpture. This is a *colour*less black-and-white-and-rust image (Steve's rusty hue is Conté crayon).

The original work is a market scene from a casbah in North Africa, with green melons and orange gourds in the left foreground. In the left background, a balcony, a mosque and a bouquet of flowers on the parapet counterbalance the foreground's circular shapes. The standing figure is an abstracted worshipper. On the right, a turban is wound round his dome-like head. Visible from behind, another figure is bent in prayer. Three alleyways of black shading distinguish the starkly lit shapes from one another. None of this rationale is known to Steve. I only learn of it later.

By 1908 the Fauvist or Wild Beasts movement was a step away from Post-Impressionism. When Henri Matisse painted this scene, it was all about light and space. Without colour, its story is camou-flaged in a photocopied (black and white) version. Nonetheless, Steve copies it (identifying with its elements). He realigns and compacts its landscape view onto a portrait-shaped paper.

Steve's passion for art, and his longing to return to it, has been buried in the impoverishment of schizophrenia and the illness's misrepresentation of reality: in how people, places and things are perceived. Yet he accurately represents multi-dimensions in this short sketch, because he is fluent in an elemental language that was the mother tongue of an artistic youth—elemental to Art—elemental to Steve.

※

I have practiced drawing exercises in Betty Edwards's *Drawing on the Right Side of the Brain*[30] on two occasions. The first time I take a course with an instructor. The second time, I'm recovering from hip-replacement surgery, and I redo all the exercises on my own, curious to discover what I missed on the first pass.

The right hemisphere of the brain is the imaginative, intuitive side, as opposed to its analytical neighbour. The two sides collaborate, yet people usually have a dominant side. In artful activities, the reason-seeking left brain can be a distraction. Edwards's exercises are designed to shut reason up, and out. She says, "In the process of learning to draw, one also learns to control how one's own brain handles information."[31] She cites George Orwell: "Probably it is better to put off using words as long as possible and get one's meaning as clear as one can through pictures or sensations."[32]

Each chapter has exercises for the student practitioner: copying portions of a drawing, copying an upside-down drawing, doing step-by-step drawings with the right or left hand (with and without looking), eyeing specific shapes and angles. It is my eye-opener to the world of art. At the time, I wasn't thinking about Steve; I was just exploring. That's what he's doing under Ann's tutelage.

One of the keys to sketch copying seems to be in *not* identifying what one is seeing. That allows the right brain to decipher the shapes and colours without the censorship of the left brain. The right brain's logical twin might ask, "Is that supposed to be a basket of melons?"

But Steve doesn't ask. He copies what he sees before him; he's at home in an artistic moment, plying one shape against another, playing all the angles.

Visual art's rule of thirds demystifies Matisse's draftsmanship (and is part of what I imagine captivates Steve). The rule divides a surface into nine squares with four intersecting power points that draw the viewer's eye. It's a game of tic-tac-toe or X's and O's, but this time, it's not about filling in the squares as game rules dictate. Rather, the four intersections are where objects of interest are placed.

The artist's intention, by virtue of composing angles and shapes (and leaving out extraneous ones), keeps the viewer's eyes dancing back and forth.

The Matisse work is a dance Steve does not sit out. He's fully engaged. The background minaret balances the worshippers' turbans and the melons in a waltz: three in the sense of the rule of thirds. One, two, three—one, two, three—minaret, turbans, melons. It is a picture dancing over power points.

An artist and former English student of mine later tells me she sees this dancing interplay in Steve's work—a fluency of line, shape, space, value and texture.

%

Steve Effervescence is a lipogram, or a Greek form of poetry that limits letter usage. Lipograms are word games or puzzles. They leave something out. I leave out all but one vowel, using the letter E, the most common letter in the English alphabet.

Greek lipogram poets left out the letter that they called a sigma or a hissing sound (it resembles an angular E). I'm reminded of stigma's hiss. I decide to skew it. The letter E has many guises in English: it can be short, as in the word *excellent*, or long, as in *need*; it can be silent (as in *sometimes*) or lazy (as in *her*) or irregular (as in *sphere*). My three-part lipogram follows a rule of thirds. Its values draw attention to the powerful points of seeing, perception—and deception.

%

Steve Effervescence I

excellent sketcher—deft welder—
needed her sphere, her germ
he-be-geezer pretense repelled
her presence deepened defense effect

elected then ejected debt
percent merger. Egress.

※

There are so many ways of seeing.

In old 1920 Al Capone movie reruns, actors like James Cagney and Edward G. Robinson had a nasal slur and a narrow vision: "It's like this, see? We rob the bank, see? Anyone who crosses me is a double crosser, see?"

There's seeing as pondering with a stroke of the chin, as in "Let... me...see."

There's "We'll see about that" indignation.

There's seeing as observing, looking and looking again, with clarity or with obscurity.

There are so many ways of seeing, if you see what I mean.

※

Steve has had glasses for as long as I can remember. Nearsightedness never minimized his love of reading. He reads everything from news-paper flyers to twenty-five-year-old mechanics' manuals. He doesn't recycle them. They amass.

The first time I notice Steve's vision (and shopping) irregularity is at the Salvation Army thrift store. He's in the change room to try on a shirt he likes; he likes it, buys it and leaves his old one behind. He then decides to see if he can stretch his luck to eyeglasses. This is how he shops.

"Let's see if I find the magic lens," says Steve.

It is a bizarre shopping technique, like a kid at an arcade trying his luck at a claw crane. He leads me to a display case (the most ex-pensive area, by Sally Ann thrift-seeking standards) with a miscellany of eyeglasses, jewellery and watches. The salesgirl is the claw. Steve's at the controls.

"Those ones," Steve points.

She swoops in to pick up the glasses he's pinpointed from a very limited selection. What are the chances he'll find his prescription? *Slim to none*, I think.

"Steve, you need your own prescription," I say.

Silence.

"Steve, why don't we get you an eye appointment?"

"NO, Joan."

※

When I make an eye appointment for myself, I get a glimmer into why he hates the idea of someone peering into his eyes. I've been fortunate, just wearing magnifying lenses for reading, but I ask my doctor if I shouldn't get my eyes checked. She agrees.

Eyes may or may not be windows to the soul, but people with schizophrenia might envision the optometrist mind reading while probing the eyes—possibly scheming to do them harm.

I wait nearly an hour in a sterile waiting room. The doctor, a stranger to me, doesn't apologize for the delay; he looks annoyed and behind schedule. Near retirement age, he seemingly can't wait to get "me" over with. Rabbit eyes examine me through periscopic equipment. His detached approach nettles me. Has Steve had appointments like this?

Perhaps this is why Steve buys glasses at thrift stores when he's feeling lucky. He sometimes wears two or three lenses at a time. He experiments with them. I give him Mum and Dad's old glasses. I've held on to them for sentimental reasons. Steve favours a lens of Mum's and holds it up to his eye like a monocle. I don't realize that this is the lucky one.

※

Ann Webborn recommends Steve come to class alone, a bit like separating mother and child. My own mum, suffering dementia in her eighties, never wanted me to leave her alone at her once-a-week eldercare. Her fear was that the "care team" would forget her in the same way she'd forgotten how she got there. I left her all the same.

On Ann's recommendation, Steve attends pottery and painting sessions without me. Other Art Studios students discover friendships and a social scene. Steve doesn't want a social scene. He doesn't qualify for an open studio to work on his own projects if he can't work collaboratively.

"Where were you today, Joan?" he says when I pick him up on the way to grocery shopping. He is implying, "You're not dumping me, are you?"

He says, "Stop signing me up."

He's done all the classes that interest him. Time to move on.

He wants Art, for Art's sake—Betty Edwards's ideal of art with a capital A. Yet I am so grateful for his reintroduction to art at the Art Studios, and to Ann and his teachers, with whom we stay in touch. Without this reintroduction to Art, Steve wouldn't have germinated his art. We're not falling off or away from one program. We're blooming Steve's art.

※

Most art programs have a teacher, yet Steve likes the self-guided approach. Any art session we find has to fit within my work schedule and fulfill Steve's Art-with-a-capital-A criteria. I look and look, and then I find what is basic.

"Life drawing is a basic inquiry into the human form,"[33] said Maurice Spira, whose quote is the mantra of a Vancouver life-drawing society, Basic Inquiry.

Basic Inquiry art studio on Main Street in Vancouver provides the venue and the equipment for drawing: easels, drawing boards, drawing horses and large clips to attach paper to board. Students bring their own drawing supplies.

I arrive early and set up the wooden horse or donkey, so called because you ride it, bareback. It has a little notch on the seat to balance a drawing board, on which I clip practice paper and acid-free paper for the three thirty-minute sketches. I put the kettle on and wait for Steve to roll in.

He brings his own supplies. He favours dollar-store paper. As time goes on, I augment it with higher-quality acid-free paper. We get art kits that look like plastic fishing tackle boxes. They sit at our feet between the drawing board and the back of the donkey. I'm no longer a bystander. In order to attend, I must draw alongside the other members in the circle.

Getting up and down from the donkey is a bit precarious. That's how his tea mug spills and breaks. The cleanup supplies are behind the bathroom door. Without making a fuss, the first time we drop and break something, I clean up. I mop up quickly. Later on, Steve does the same.

///

"Where's my lens?" Steve asks as we are getting into the car after a session.

"What lens?"

"Joan, you swept up the broken bits."

"That was the mug; I never saw a lens."

"Go back and find it."

He is annoyed. I'm not thrilled. The manager and model are wrapping up for the day; the model is collecting her cheque.

"I don't like going through garbage, Steve."

"Just find it, Joan. You lost my lucky lens."

"Hey, are you two siblings?" asks the model.

"Yeah," I reply.

"Cool. You bicker like siblings."

She distracts us from the intensity of the moment. I do not find the lucky lens. I do not persuade Steve to get an eye appointment.

Matisse cites Picasso, "Painting is a blind man's profession. He paints not what he sees, but what he feels, what he tells himself about what he has seen."[34]

This is where Steve wants to go with Art. He's feeling his way.

※

Steve Effervescence II

secret-seven sped, stretched
peppered eggshells. eked endless effect.
see them. there. velvet veneer where

hell smelt—leer felt fermented.
nevertheless, she met regret.
wheedled fettered webs.

※

Contour detection is one visual abnormality I observe when Steve draws over the edges of two overlapping pieces of paper, or when the charcoal moves from paper to drawing board so that the figure is bisected. Doesn't he know the charcoal is careening off the edge? Is he so single-minded he doesn't care? I think the intensity of his focus takes the figure off the page. I don't realize it's unconscious.

Steve does full-figure representations as well as portraits or head-and-shoulder views. His likenesses don't always capture the model's expression. His faces are classical and remind me of the framed reproductions of Renaissance Madonnas that Mum had on my bedroom walls—sombre with eyes downcast.

Models can't smile cheerily and hold that expression for a thirty-minute pose. Their faces are neutral. Steve's faces are neutral, including his own. What comes out on paper is unique in line, form and composition. Steve's work is powerful, colourful and vital. That he can't see fine detail doesn't dawn on me.

Another visual defect is sensitivity to colour, hue and light. Sensitivity to light can cause blurriness, enough to cause lightheadedness. It can trigger hallucinations, complete with moving parts. In art, this can be a gift. In life, it can be frightful.

※

After a session at Basic Inquiry, we're sitting outdoors at an eatery we've been to before. We order sandwiches. Some workmen are seated about twenty paces away, behind Steve. The mid-afternoon sun is behind me. Is the sun in Steve's eyes? He becomes agitated and looks at me as if I am a demon. An orc sighting. He kicks the chair and shouts something unintelligible. Something has thrown him into the dumpster without Bilbo's ring for protection. The workmen look concerned, ready to intervene. I keep my voice steady.

"Steve, I'm going home now. See you next week. Please take your medication." I don't know what else to say, even though lithium doesn't prevent psychoses. He is not on antipsychotic meds. Dr. P told me lithium "slows down his engine." Today, his engine is overheating.

Steve looks relieved but distracted. I am rattled. He walks home, about a mile, or maybe he takes a bus. I never find out. A social worker later tells me that I did the right thing, removing myself from a tenuous situation. This is not the brother I know. This is the illness. I hate this uninvited visitor who has spoiled our day—has spoiled Steve's life.

Steve has the intervening week, and the years dealing with psychoses, to gather his thoughts. Art is on the line. He doesn't want to blight this relationship. It is ours, in its fledgling stage.

Steve is also in a stage, known as phase three (ages fifty-five to sixty-four), of schizophrenia where the positive symptoms (psychoses, hallucination and delusion) are in decline. Burnout. That time frame corresponds with our time together. Steve doesn't want our relationship to dissolve into an orc nightmare. Willing it won't make hallucinations go away. Perhaps it is that Middle-earthling mid-life that J.R.R. Tolkien referred to that has got the demons on the run. In a way, our time framework is our lucky lens.

※

I dream of someone familiar to me. (I forget whom, because my conscious brain can't remember.) I accept that it is she, even though her face is altered. The dream unfolds like a movie, and I take in the situation as it develops. She is my friend. Dream rules allow for that. Steve's reality allows for face smudging, even facial distortion.

Some nights when I turn off the bedside light, a residual image remains in the pixels behind my eyelids, an image resembling a face, a pleasant face, one that can change to a less pleasant one in milliseconds—from benign to grotesque.

Another night, just as I begin to fall asleep, a nightmare is brewing. It's as if acid is thrown over a glass image, streaking and bubbling. A tooth dream is coming on, in which I lose all my teeth in one gummy variation after another. They don't fall out. I pull them out in globs.

Dream analyzers suggest radical changes are in the works for those who have this dream, or that I'm about to let go of something. I recognize the source of this troubling dream. That's not a privilege Steve has. How does he explain what and how he sees: real-time, daytime nightmares?

As Mum's advocate when she had some decayed teeth removed, I sat with her at the dentist's surgery, reassured her, reminded her why she was there and watched the slow injection of needles. "It's because of her age," explained the dentist. "The freezing must be injected slowly." Her teeth were extracted and her gums packed with gauze. When we left the surgery, she couldn't remember what had happened.

"Mum, you've had teeth removed to make room for a nice new set." She loved getting new teeth. I dream about all the ways mine might fall out.

※

Steve Effervescence III
teethed sweetness whenever elders wept.
slept ere wretchedness
leeched bled weeds.
fewer fences, lesser pretense.
swept seeds wherever. we three: he, me, them.
we've seen the cleft ebb: the perfect tercet.

※

Charcoal is a medium that dates back twenty-three thousand years and was used in body painting. Steve holds the rich, dark stump over his sketch paper. This finely ground organic material is his wedge on reality. It is on his hands, on his face, under his nails, in his tea, in his coffee. It is black and smudgy, and he prefers it to felt markers or Sharpies, as a finishing outline. He doesn't wash his hands afterwards. It marks him, but not like a stigma—it is his craftsman's badge. He looks like a coal miner, fresh from a shift.

Edges, outlines and details aren't part of his visual field. He uses charcoal outlines to bookend the work and ground it: black is his charcoal anchor.

Less obvious is how easily charcoal can be lifted or erased, particularly if it isn't bound by wax or gum. Without a binder, it is free. What a tool to begin self-expression—and what freedom of expression.

April 2011, chalk pastel, Conté crayon and charcoal.

Circa 2013, chalk pastel, Conté crayon, charcoal and acrylic.

February 2011, chalk pastel, Conté crayon and charcoal.

June 2011, chalk pastel, Conté crayon and charcoal.

Circa 2013, chalk pastel, Conté crayon and charcoal.

February 2011, chalk pastel, Conté crayon and charcoal.

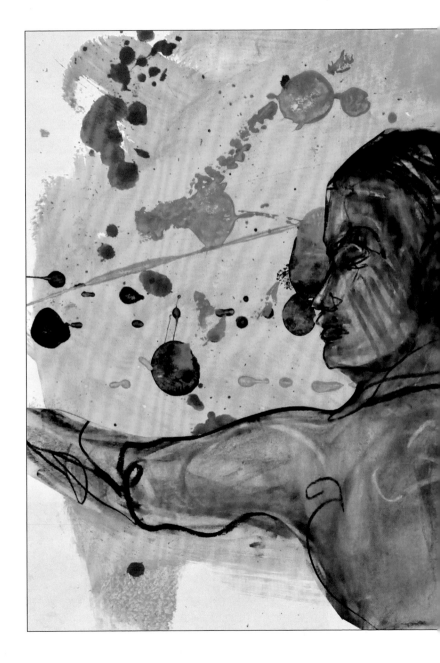

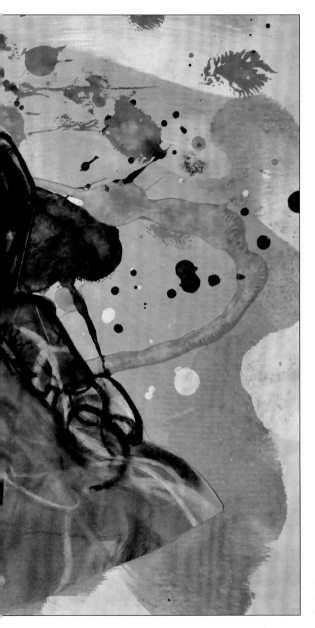

October 2010, chalk pastel,
Conté crayon, charcoal and
acrylic.

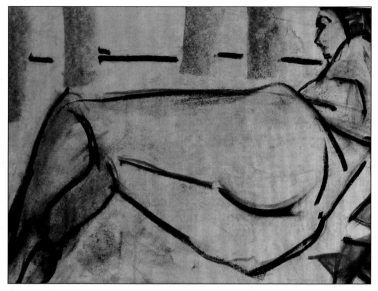

March 2011, chalk pastel, Conté crayon and charcoal.

May 2011, chalk pastel, Conté crayon and charcoal.

Circa 2013, chalk pastel, Conté crayon and charcoal.

October 2012, chalk
pastel, Conté crayon
and charcoal.

Circa 2013, chalk pastel, Conté crayon and charcoal.

Circa 2013, chalk pastel, Conté crayon and charcoal.

August 2011, chalk pastel,
Conté crayon and charcoal.

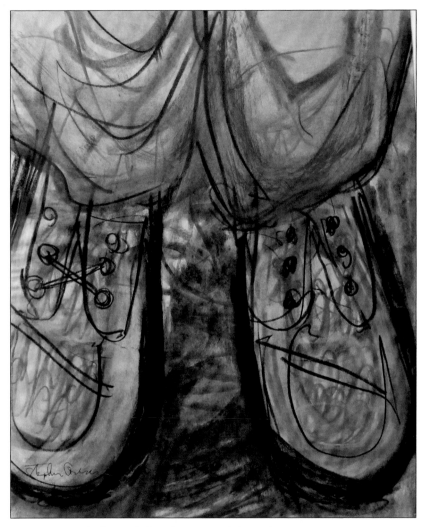

February 2011, chalk pastel, Conté crayon and charcoal.

CHAPTER 5

Ruler and Tape Measure

DARREN HAS A SET of bocce balls that he lends Steve and me—a long-term loan. I stash them in one of Steve's many carrier bags on the back floor of the car—the khaki-orange bag on wheels with an outside pocket for a tape measure. Eight balls (four red, four green) make a heavy haul. Each ball weighs two pounds or 920 grams. The bag's wheels buffer the load when I swing it in and out of the car on its retractable handle.

Bocce winds down our Tuesdays after art and errands. It's a ball game. In most weather, most seasons, we go to any of a half-dozen parks near Steve's home and play. A relatively flat and grassy surface is fair game. Steve is drawn to the 130-acre Queen Elizabeth Park, along its north and northeast flanks. Vancouverites call this park Little Mountain.

Official bocce courts are long rectangles, and we play the traditional way, on natural grounds. Less traditional is the way we move around the field of play. We superimpose our rectangle over the ten ends or twelve accrued points (whichever arrives first), starting where the car is parked, and then returning to it. Toss, play and move. Whoever wins the last end determines the direction of the next.

Just before I was born, our family lived on Cambie Street, across from Queen Elizabeth Park. I'm told that Mum waved good night from the nearby pediatric hospital's postnatal unit, where she bore us. Her hospital room faced our backyard.

Dad must have known when to orchestrate the wave. Rod waved back at Mum and baby Darren. Then it was toddler Darren's turn, with Rod, to wave back at Mum and baby Steve, a year and four months later. The three preschoolers might have waved from the yard when the twins arrived. By the time I arrived, the family had moved west of our umbilical Cambie Street root. Steve now lives ten minutes away to the southeast. I'm to the northwest, across Burrard Inlet and up a mountain.

Queen Elizabeth Park is a high point in Vancouver, with a cemented-in reservoir at its pinnacle—a 175-million-litre capacity repository for Vancouver's drinking-water supply. For Steve and me, it is an oasis—our bocce refuge.

Every week we troll the neighbourhood for bocce grounds; we make our choice depending on the weather, the season, the allotted time, parking spots and who's around.

"Here?" I suggest.

"No, let's go to Queen E," Steve invariably says.

McDonald Park is our smallest venue. Several tennis courts skirt its eastern boundary; a children's playground is to the west. We play along the tennis court periphery. Our shots roll against the raised barrier.

Columbia Park is double McDonald Park's size and my default park when time is short. A large baseball diamond is central to the park. The diamond itself is too gravelly for bocce, although bocce balls roll faster over it. From here, we can see the North Shore Mountains. From here, the sky is a vast Etch A Sketch, with white jet streams from airplanes leaving YVR marking its empty blue scorecard.

Bocce Pantoum I

You toss; heads or tails?
Choose your colour—red or green
Throw the "jack," that little white marker,
To determine the length of the end.
Choose your colour—red or green
Stop & start—keep moving
To determine the length of the end
In this bocce-ball game of life.

※

For us, Queen Elizabeth Park is the queen of bocce parks. Arboretum pines, spruce and fir dot the greens. These trees are the same age as Steve, planted in 1949 along her north-facing slopes.

I chase a rolling bowl down that slope onto a busy street. I scoop the bowl out of the gutter as cars speed by.

"Steve, this bocce court is too steep," I say. He likes varied terrain, but I draw the line.

We shift our court to a more level grove of trees, but the carpet of grass is choked with roots, branch debris, cones and needles. We move again to the eastern side, the Ontario Street Frisbee-golf area. We play bocce when few Frisbee golfers are there, in the early afternoon. We play on the edge of the dog walkers' zone, until I wonder: "What is this, stuck on the boule? Mud, or...?"

We find quiet picnic spots (and bring hand wipes) around Queen Elizabeth's Quarry Garden, the Bloedel Floral Conservatory, the bowling green and the Henry Moore sculpture *Knife Edge: Two Piece*—one of four full-sized bronze casts worldwide. We rip open a sourdough loaf, slice into roasted chicken (I've moved from pescatarian to flexitarian) and add a dollop of coleslaw for good measure.

Steve loves Henry Moore's *Knife Edge*. He squeezes between the two pieces, hammers on them with his fists and listens to the echo against the paved plaza and nearby fountains that sputter an intermittent sixty-five-jet rhythm.

Henry Moore was a twentieth-century British sculptor who freed the genre from traditional ties and returned it to more primitive roots. He vouched for artwork that had "a vitality of its own…independent of the object it represents…deeper than the senses…a penetration into reality…an expression of the significance of life."[35]

The fact that Steve and the two Henrys, Henry Moore and Henri Matisse, vitalize their art in this way comes to me later. Steve's unwitting connection with these artists puts him in an artistic stream— the current or vein of Art, tapping into it.

Moore said, "The human figure is the basis of all my sculptures, and that for me means the female nude…50 to 1."[36]

Steve aligns with Matisse's view that "what interests me most is neither still life nor landscape, but the human figure. It is that which best permits me to express my almost religious awe towards life."[37]

I give Steve a book called *Paintings That Changed the World: From Lascaux to Picasso*.[38] In it, drawings of semi-clothed figures feature at the throne of Tutankhamen in the 1300s BCE, with the young ruler's wife anointing him. A Greek flute player from a fifth-century-BCE fresco. The Bayeux Tapestry's Norman and Saxon soldier figures fight it out in 1066 on fifty panels or scenes. Botticelli's *The Birth of Venus*. Michelangelo's *The Creation of Adam*. Mythological and military; royal and religious—all figures come together. Lounging women in Turkish baths; Seurat's boy bathers—detailed and distorted, proportional and disproportional, nude and layered in costumes, uniforms, drapery and regalia.

Many artists at Basic Inquiry do other genres of art in other mediums. I've seen Basic artists' *plein-air* (open-air landscape) work in acrylic, oil and watercolour paint at the North Shore's "Art in the Garden" tour, or at the Eastside Culture Crawl, an annual visual arts, design and crafts festival. Steve would dally and deviate from figure drawing too, if he could. However, getting to Basic is as much organization as he can muster. Plus, Basic is at the heart of our hometown: Main Street, dividing Vancouver with an east-west artery.

"Steve, figurative art matters. It's the bulk of what this book calls the best," I say.

The Tate weighs in on figurative art, suggesting it "retains strong references to the real world and particularly to the human figure."[39]

Steve needs strong references to the real world.

%

Bocce Pantoum II

Stop & start—keep moving
Toss it underhand
In this bocce-ball game of life
Be a role model.

Toss it underhand:
That little white marker.
Be a roll model as you
Toss—heads or tails?

%

Steve's peers at Basic Inquiry are excited about his work, saying, "So loose and expressive!" They don't say it directly to him (ducking a tempest). They say it within earshot, or take me aside and say so.

The intimacy of drawing nudes is all-embracing. Taking off one's coat, then one's sweater, opening one's self to the process (with regard to the model), and I say this figuratively, since Steve rarely removes any layers.

The drawing tools trace the tender curve of a shoulder, a calf muscle, a breast. The artists' hands communicate without confusion, like an attentive lover. Steve might as well be sculpting or carving the model. At the same time, he's shedding layers to the core of his being, finding his own vanishing point.

%

The coin toss determines who throws the little white ball, target or jack. The "jack" is a bocce and a lawn bowling term. Mum and Dad were both lawn bowling aficionados. Dad was a three-time Canadian champ in the fours; Mum won the Canadian Women's Championship in pairs and triples. Bowling (boule is French for bowl) sports are familiar to the seven of us Corks, even if we play rarely; we were familiar with Mum and Dad's play.

Steve and I play three or four games. The closest bowls to the jack win. If my bowl is closest, it's the winner. If I have the second, third or fourth closest bowl, I win up to four consecutive points per end, no more. That's another of our bent-bocce rules. The bending of rules evolves in how we relax ourselves and the rules as we go.

Four bowls each. I give up winning the toss when I opt for colour: red over green. The red ones are easier to see. Green boules blend with the grass, and we nearly always play on grass, or some semblance of it. As Steve's eyesight fails, I hold up a shiny marker behind the jack. Later yet, I stand behind it, marking its position, like a buoy.

The main difference between lawn bowling and bocce for us is that we needn't join a club or go to a manicured bowling green. The bocce bowls are round, unlike elliptical lawn bowling balls. They are pitched underhand in the manner of softball play. Lawn bowls have an *in* bias and an *out* bias. Bocce bowls have no bias. We like that.

On rainy days, we choose a well-drained pitch instead of the water-soaked lowland. Squelching noises deter from drawing to the jack. Colour saturation is elemental in the vividness of a hue, but shoe saturation?

Steve adjusts the length of the bocce end. He has more strength than me. If he throws a long end, I can't bowl that far. He keeps it within my reach, just. Winning is important to him. In fact it makes his day. He discusses match points with his psychiatrist. He tells me so. Game strategy is important in their artful discussions. They discuss the art—of bocce. I wonder what a monthly bocce report sounds like with Doctor P. Maybe a bit like Mum's lawn bowling replays.

※

Mum took up lawn bowling in her sixties. She became an expert pairs player in her seventies. She would return home and recap the game, end by end, shot by shot—how it unfolded, the ups and downs, the ins and outs.

"I drew to the jack. Then Ethel threw a guard to protect my bowl. I got in another one. What a shot she made. We checked the head to find we were lying shot."

"Great, Mum." We'd stifle a yawn.

Ethel was Mum's partner. I have a photo of them accepting championship medals from Mike Harcourt, Vancouver's mayor at the time. Dad, on the other hand, would simply say whether he'd won or not. No need to ask. The win was discernible from the triumphant glow. The loss—a black cloud. Steve is a mix of Mum and Dad's post-game reactions. He details like Mum and wears the "thrill of victory and agony of defeat"[40] expression of Dad's post-game response.

We watched ABC's *Wide World of Sports* every Saturday as kids. The newsreel that opened the program showed the thrills of one athlete being lifted onto the shoulders of adoring fans, of receiving a gold medal or of power lifting a world-record weight. In contrast, an infamous Slovenian ski jumper, Vinko Bogataj, crashed his landing. The commentator, Jim McKay, coined the phrase "the thrill of victory and the agony of defeat."

※

I try to win, yet I am not as strategic as Steve. Some days the luck is with me. I am sorry to beat him, but I won't rig the game. I keep track of the score in the same way Steve did in his teenaged tennis matches with Darren. I call out the score after each play to prevent any uncertainty. Direct and fair. That's the deal. Halfway through a game, he or I might be down a few shots.

"It's not over till it's over," I say.

If he pulls out a win under those circumstances, he can't hide his pleasure. A come-from-behind victory is sweet—a *Wide World of Sports* moment.

Close ends necessitate tape measuring. We walk down to examine the configuration of bowls, size it up. He holds one end of the tape and I read, or more often, I hold the hook end and he reads. I don't mind losing a game to win a brother.

"Pull it taut, Joan!" Steve commands.

One sunny spring day, he pulls off a come-from-behind victory. In jubilation, he pulls out a toothbrush and squats down to pose. But first, he rearranges the boules into a red-boule happy face— green eyes and nose, a white-toothed Jack. He is declaring a win for the day, so very pleased with himself. He rarely poses for a photograph. McDonald Park—tiebreaker comeback. I'm sure it plays out in sessions with Dr. P.

That toothbrush has been an accessory of Steve's ever since he had dental work a year earlier. He carries it with him, pulling it out at the most inopportune moments. "I'm glad you're taking care of your teeth, Steve," I say, hoping he'll stop frothing his way across the parking lot.

Some days, he uses his considerable strength to fire the jack, one of Dad's specialty lawn bowling shots, also known as the drive shot. It burns the end or explodes a hopeless configuration of bowls around the jack. There is a fifty-fifty chance they'll explode in your favour. They might explode in mine. Taking out bowls at great speed was Dad's style: his fiery temperament. In lawn bowls, as in curling and billiards and life, it breaks it all up.

After a few of Steve's failed burnt-end drives, I say, "You're a good drawer...why don't you just draw to the jack?" A realization dawns on both of us. He draws. He's a drawer—one that draws.

Steve knows he is not his father's son. That fieriness doesn't jive with his gentle nature. Drawing is his ability and his art form. Drawing in bocce ball games is different from drawing with sketch tools, but it is an appealing word play. Drawing: artful training. Drawing to the jack: coming closer to the target. He's doing both.

%

We went to the Coast Mental Health Clubhouse in 2004. Their focus was pre-vocational and vocational training for employment through the development of social and work skills. What could Steve do in his mid-fifties, having been unemployed and unemployable since his thirties? In a way, he was homebound, except for the fact he could walk, shop and subsist.

From 2005 until 2007, we became members of the Art Studios. We transitioned to Basic Inquiry several years before the idea of a solo show materialized. I submitted his pieces in Basic Inquiry Members' Shows with his knowledge that I was doing it in a managerial role. It took a year to collect (persuade and coerce) fifty-seven pieces for his first show.

I learn enough about Steve's routines to know that he, who was sociable in his teens, no longer has friends. His social interactions take place through shopping and running errands. To benefit from being with a group without socializing is to be in a common activity.

"I don't like people," he says one day after the art session ends.

I've heard him say this before. I am hoping the reason he tells me is that I am becoming the exception.

%

The air is fresh, and we are walking and bowling—checking boule configurations. When we do, Steve's interactions seem normal. He doesn't rant; there's no time for that. The activity is focused. Structure is built in, same as sketch time.

Bocce is now more than a game. It is give and take (bowling in turns), a connection we share. Through bocce play, we are filling negative spaces (those spaces in art that surround, define and bring balance to the image); negative space is defined more by the background than by the main figure. We're pulling focus from the main figure, all the while supporting it. Hurray to that.

≋

In an English lesson with my adult ESL students, we leave the classroom for the softball field adjacent to the learning centre. We are going to play scrub. I've mapped out the baseball diamond on the whiteboard. Positions: batter, pitcher, backcatcher, shortstop, base keepers and outfielders, dotting the field of play.

We've reviewed the simple rules of scrub baseball, a game in which the fielders work their way from outfield to infield in an S-formation, flowing through the positions, making their way up to bat. We're all on the same team; we're trying every position—batter, runner, outfielder. Every time there's an out, the players move one position in the S. The lesson is about fair play and small talk. Positivity reinforces positive relationships, which keep the conversation moving forward. But it's a lot bigger than that.

Expressions like *way to go, good shot, well played, fantastic, super, well done, try again, better luck next time* and *bad luck* work their way into Steve's and my bocce jargon. They trickle into real-life conversations. We practice it. We apply it.

You lucky sod. You dirty rat. It is all in the tone.

If Steve and I tie two games, we go to a tiebreaker, with a picnic in between. I pack folding chairs. Dog walkers look on, curious.

Everyone loves a game, especially John Nash, whose 1994 Nobel Prize in Economic Science was based on game theory: "Games...involve one kind of interdependence. The players move in sequence, each aware of the other's moves...looking ahead to every possible outcome."[41]

※

Tape measures are flexible rulers. They signify fairness and exactitude. They've been used in mathematics, technical drawing, printing, surveying and tailoring to calibrate line and measure distance since a Mesopotamian straightedge was found at an excavation site, dating to 2650 BCE.

Canada went metric in the early 1970s, with measurement of distance and speed, height and weight; with cooking measurements and temperatures; with food, drink and packaged products. Metric measurement measures metres to the order of a milli, centi or kilo magnitude, whereas imperial measurement measures inches and feet. Canadian baby boomers such as us are bilingual in a bi-numeral culture. A tape measure's function seems entirely error-proof, but its accuracy does depend upon which end you're at—how you use numeration and whether you report the reading accurately.

Ours is a sixteen-foot or five-metre ruler. What we are measuring extends well beyond its scope.

CHAPTER 6

Pastels

I ARRIVE AT BASIC INQUIRY at 9:30 by car from North Vancouver to set up Steve's space. And mine. The session manager arrives early with the key to open up. Basic Inquiry life-drawing sessions are Tuesdays, 10:00 a.m. to 1:00 p.m. That's time enough for a marathon-running event, which is how I perceive the length of these sessions. Until I get in the groove. Steve's in the groove from the get-go.

Basic Inquiry session managers are accomplished artists in their own right. Bernie is a photographer; Elizabeth is a potter and fabric artist; James is a sculptor.

The session manager ensures that the model arrives and gets paid, that the artist members pay for each session, that everyone cleans up after themselves and that enough donkeys and easels are accessible. The artists self-regulate everything else.

I clip paper to an angled sketch board, allowing a clear view of the model. I don't spectate these sessions as I did at the Art Studios. I lay out the drawing tools between us. I am still Steve's advocating go-between—a cross between a donkey and a horse: his mule.

These are artists' sessions. They aren't classes. They aren't instructional. Steve has learned to focus at the Art Studios (Darren's shut-up-and-draw decree), and he now makes good use of Basic's time structure. He's in his element. At these new sessions, we sketch one model in multiple poses—the same format every time. It has a quiet predictability.

The room's one supporting pillar provides a buffer for Steve. I position myself next to him. We're in a circular formation around the yet-to-arrive model. I print off the model timetable ahead of time for Steve and myself. Most times, we wait to find out who it is: male or female, tall or short, lean or stocky.

Initially, it's a struggle for me. A blues poem caps it:

My Schizophrenia Blues

I don't have it; I'm just a fragment
Of what he has: a torrent
Of ill-begotten psychoses.

Steve arrives by bicycle with full panniers, or by bus with a buggy or valise, chockablock with Value Village goodie bags of crayons, felts. Some dollar-store paper. When he arrives, I let him settle in without more than a "Hi Steve." I've learned that much from Mr. Sharpie.

He brings coffee and snacks, as well as books and magazines that he's saved for design ideas. He tapes clippings from home, garden or fashion glossies to his drawing board. A makeup or style ad might have caught his eye.

I don't think the subscription to *Canadian Art* magazine is that important until it runs out.

"Where's the art magazine this month?" he asks.

"Okay, Steve. I'll re-subscribe you."

"You're the manager, Joan."

The artists all have slightly different perspectives, determined by their vantage point in the circle. The model moves one way and then another to accommodate front-on, side-on and back-view poses. No one wants all posterior views. The warm-up consists of three-, five- and ten-minute sketches, which build from gestural drawings to three thirty-minute compositions.

There are two twenty-minute breaks when members stretch, chat or have a snack. I keep replenishing Steve's morning coffee with tea for less caffeine, less agitation. Steve starts bringing snacks like pineapple, cheese and crackers, even a cucumber. He directs me to serve them at the break, while he continues sketching. Does he get me to serve treats to limit his own interaction? Or does he enjoy watching me distribute his gifts? Does he observe (peripherally) how they are received?

"Would you like some?" I cut snacks into bite-sized bits and circulate, like I did with a dessert tray of pastries at my first waitress job.

"Oh, thanks for bringing these, Joan," they say. "Delicious."

"These are from Steve," I say.

James, the manager, picks up the food-sharing tradition. Food is such a people-knitter.

Steve gives me some of his homemade muffins to take home. I find a chicken bone in one. Some are so stale they feel like grenades. I give him my treasured muffin cookbook, but he never brings any to the session. Those recipes call for baking powder, baking soda or a little of both. He's in love with yeast as a leavening agent from his bread-, beer- and wine-making days.

"I already had a bowl of porridge this morning," I say. Or "I'm not that hungry right now, Steve."

"Throw them to the crows on your way home," he says.

He hands over store-bought pastries for me to heat up. Microwave ovens are a new technology for him, but he warms to it.

Artists drift in, choose a seat and saddle up their donkeys for the three-hour session. The model arrives and disrobes in the washroom.

I don't have it; I'm merriment—
Entertainment
Through a harsh diagnosis.

The female model strips down to a light robe; the male model might have a towel wraparound and a tee-shirt. Once they step up onto the locked-wheel platform, they let loose all garments. The robe, towel or covering sometimes becomes an accessory, drawn into the sketch or draped around the model or the stool on which they perch.

That moment of model uncovering is like a conductor raising his baton. We orchestra members sit taller and put drawing tool to paper, like bows to violins. Chatter ceases. The eye adjusts to the form at hand. It is time to pick up instruments and, instead of playing within the seven-note scale, we play with Art's seven elements.

Steve's work is impressionistic, bold. Every piece is his. Every piece has his intangible, distinctive brand. What is it? There's a certainty in every stroke that I try to copy. He doesn't look at me, speak to me or judge my efforts, but he is teaching me nonetheless—silently showing me his artistic self, and more indirectly, an artistic path—open to all.

In an early blog, I explore what I see as his fluidity with the art form. An artist looks at our two pieces and says, "Look at the fluidity in this piece [Steve's] as compared to that one. Sorry, is that yours?"

I have to laugh. I'm an impostor, but thanks to Steve, I'm along for the ride.

William Kluba describes how stimulating it is to be a beginner. I am that beginner. And Steve is beginning again.

"We are discovering ourselves without fear," says Kluba. "Seeing in art is quite different than normal seeing...the act of understanding through practice and awareness. Your perceptions become heightened and attuned to the art and ready to engage in the work...through shape, line, and negative space....We train our eyes [and]...it changes the way we see the world."[42]

I've learned from *Drawing on the Right Side of the Brain*[43] classes, inspired by Betty Edwards's book of the same name, that the right brain finds awareness without words. As a holistic puzzler, the right brain is looking for ways to put the whole together, noticing similarities. Without reasoning, it is intuitive, spatial and timeless.

※

Let it vent;
This vent that's never spent.
Spilling out in supportable doses.

As for viewing art, Steve and I attend several art exhibits at the Vancouver Art Gallery. The most influential, pertaining to his work, is *The Modern Woman: Drawings by Degas, Renoir, Toulouse-Lautrec and Other Masterpieces from the Musée d'Orsay* in the summer of 2010. It sets a tone for Steve's first exhibit: *Dancing on the Interface*, set for February, six months hence.

The Musée d'Orsay has permitted this nineteenth-century French art collection to leave Paris for the first time. I preview it once for my own enjoyment.

The exhibit's curator, Isabelle Julia, reveals how artists' individuality and intimacy are expressed: "The artist…sought out emotions and ideas that spoke to the personality not only of the subject but also of the individual creating the work. To draw is to make manifest the deep inner self that allows one to grasp an object in all its permutations."[44]

A second time to the exhibit, I bring Steve after our session at Basic. I track him as he moves restlessly and rapidly through the gallery. We grab a snack on the café terrace after the first go-round and then move through again, more slowly. Is he picking up on artistic expression in the way the curator cited?

Is he relating to Degas's pastel ladies at their toilet (bath), or the peasants at work in the fields, or the café scenes? Lasting impressions are contrasted and highlighted in Seurat's figures. The use of pen and ink enhances the outline in Bourdelle's *Female Nude*, or his sketch *Isadora Duncan Dancing*.

Are Steve's impressions taking form?

For me, Degas's *Standing Nude with Left Leg Raised* and his rendering of his friend, fellow artist and oft-times model Mary Cassatt in *Young Woman Tying Her Hat Ribbons* are impressive. But there are others, like Berthe Morisot's *Half-Nude Woman Fixing Her Hair*, Vuillard's *Seated Nude Model* and Renoir's *Seated Bather Drying Her Arms*. All communicate something from the inner self of the model to the inner self of the artist to the viewer's perception. A mind-soul-spirit connection surfaces.

A flurry of inspiration leaves Steve going into a productive fall.

%

That fall of 2010, I continue to buy supplies from a variety of art stores. Steve and I occasionally shop together. Acid-free paper and practice paper pads, chalk pastels, markers, erasers, Conté crayons, charcoal sticks and applicators are our bits and pieces.

I have some worries about the pastel medium. Chalk pastels are made from pure pigment. The most toxic are the three Cs: chromium greens, reds and yellows; cobalt blues; cadmium yellows and reds. Steve breaks all rules for their use: Avoid inhaling dust. Work outside. Wash hands frequently or wear gloves. If Steve wears rubber gloves, the reused ones quickly get worn and torn.

I consider the toxicity of his hoarder's house and let it go.

I don't have this brain-disease-bent
That's all I'm saying; that's what I meant,
Nor its pains and losses.

Uncovered beverages that rest at Steve's feet get a dusting of pastel chalk.

"Let me dump this coffee, Steve," I say.

"No, Joan; don't waste it."

"Steve, I'll make you a fresh one." The fresh one is the gentler drink—tea.

This tactic is part of what I learned with my aging parents. Better not to ask; just do it. I dump the pastel powder down the sink.

How Steve starts with pastels is as Hazel Harrison alludes: "A child takes the first steps in art with chalks or crayons rather than paint and brushes, relishing the ease of spreading color on paper," and, "Pastel painting...is both a drawing and a painting medium. The stick of color becomes virtually an extension of your hand: just as the child does, you can pick it up and start painting."[45]

Harrison goes on to say, "Pastel versatility, and its easy handling...[make it the] most direct of all media....[From] sweeping side strokes for broad impressions and line strokes for more precise portrayals...colours [blend] into rich mixtures...hazy effects for which the medium is so well-suited."[46]

I learn and imitate from the other artists, but mostly from Steve, who is one of only a few using pastel sticks. It takes me back to hopscotch patterns drawn on sidewalks or blacktopped playgrounds. Pastels are as smooth and spreadable as sugar icing. We use pastel ovals with applicator sticks, spreading the medium on practice paper and acid-free white paper, and on tinted paper or Mi-Teintes, with enough tooth and texture to allow rubbing and blending.

Harrison adds, "A gray or beige paper allows you to judge both the light and the dark colors, because it provides a middle tone....Pastel is a partnership between pigment and paper [to] enhance the work."[47]

I calculate how many pieces of practice paper we need for the initial three-to-ten-minute poses, and I allow four pieces of better-quality paper for the final three. Steve uses both sides.

"How much did you pay for that paper, Joan?"

"This isn't dollar-store paper, Steve. You pay a bit more for quality." I order the tinted paper, delivered free to my doorstep with a minimum shipment of five pads or more.

Steve reminds me that I am on his budget and not to splurge on supplies. I remind him that I too know how to find good deals. *Bien sur, we bicker like siblings*, I smile to myself.

With damp, soapy paper towels, I wipe his forehead between rounds of art, like he's a boxer between rounds. He sips tea and keeps drawing. Thirty-minute compositions stretch into forty-five minutes to an hour or more.

According to Harrison, "strokes made with the tip or edge...can be infinitely varied...long, light strokes; short, jabbing ones; curves and dots...from light to heavy, or from fine to thick...blended or unblended... gestural marks....One line is drawn over another in free and rapid movements of the hand and wrist....The impression of movement, and the network of lines rather than one line alone creates the image."[48]

In Harrison's view, "painting is a process of constant evaluation. You need to keep the entire image fluid so that you can make changes as you work[49]...create relationships...of color, of shape, of technique, or of all three[50]...repeating colors...shapes...unity of technique [yet] an element of contrast."[51]

Steve is experimenting with stroke angles and edges of chalk pastels, charcoal and Conté sticks. The line is something he is finding, like a path. He is exploring—finding truth along the way.

※

Steve has a copy of Kimon Nicolaides' *The Natural Way to Draw*, often considered the bible of art training. He has underlined passages:

"Imagine that your pencil point is touching the model instead of the paper."[52]

"Be guided more by the sense of touch than by sight."[53]

"Keep the whole thing going at once."[54]

He's juggling. His inner clown is happy.

"Drawing depends on seeing. Seeing depends on knowing.... Add feeling and thought."[55]

When I persuade Steve to give me the finished product, I use a light fixative to preserve the finish. The pieces move to the Corcoran Gallery, ground zero at my home. My home gallery: named after a defunct one in Washington, DC, whose namesake, William Corcoran, was a wealthy banker.

When Steve hoards pieces, they don't survive the grime and the wear and tear of his home.

※

"Why don't you think about having a member's show, Steve?" says Shelley, a Basic model, art teacher and practicing artist. Steve looks overwhelmed and doesn't reply.

He doesn't refuse when I start collecting pieces. I want to put them in frames, under glass, to protect them.

"Humph," he says, handing me the two I ask for.

"You do the art, Steve. That's your job. I'll do the rest."

I don't have it, but let him vent
Reality in its current
Incarnating prognosis.

Respect and praise are new to him. It depends who offers it and Steve's frame of mind. If someone says they like something he's done, so what? If they hate it, so what? Steve's approach to praise and blame seems that he wants to live outside social ideals or judgment. Blame simmers resentment. But praise? Praise is harder to reject. One new member at Basic tells Steve he likes his work, and Steve nearly explodes. A young female model tells him she likes his work, and he gives the piece to her.

%

In Kenneth Clark's *The Nude: A Study in Ideal Form*, Clark suggests that the nude (not the one in *Playboy* magazine fold-outs, but the classic nude figure) is "the human body...turned into art...[that] is ourselves, and arouses memories of all things we wish to do with ourselves."[56]

"Steve, is it okay if we draw nudes?" I had asked Steve this question when we began life-drawing sessions at Basic Inquiry.

"I went to art school, Joan."

As if that summed it up.

In a class inspired by Betty Edwards, the instructor suggested I continue my practice with life drawing. My Catholic upbringing wouldn't allow for it at that time. Always concealing more than revealing, for modesty's sake.

I'll never do that, I thought. *Too embarrassing.* (By "do that," I meant "sketch nudes.")

Steve's artistic need and the necessity for a flexible schedule lead us to Basic Inquiry's life-drawing sessions.

After one of our art sessions, Steve and I prowl Granville Street galleries. I ask a proprietor why there aren't more nudes or figure drawings for sale in and around Vancouver. Life drawing as a practice is taking off, but not sales.

"Nudes are an urban genre," explains the owner. "You'll see more of them in Montreal or Toronto. Westerners are fixated on land-scapes...maybe it's all our mountain-sea-sky views."

Kenneth Clark, man of letters and defender of the nude, explains it best: "To be naked is to be deprived of our clothes, and the word implies some of the embarrassment most of us feel in that condition. The word *nude*, on the other hand, carries...no uncomfortable overtone. The vague image it projects into the mind is not of a huddled and defenseless body, but of a balanced, prosperous, and confident body."[57]

Clark says, "The Greeks perfected the nude in order that man might feel like a god....We still feel close to divinity in those flashes of self-identification when, through our own bodies, we seem to be aware of a universal order."[58]

Long before Greek gods, heroes and athletes, Eve and Adam became aware of their nakedness in the Garden of Eden. Clark mentions a biblical reference: "The Word was made flesh, and dwelt among us...full of grace and truth."[59]

As far as female nudity, Spartan women exposed more than their thighs in wrestling competitions that Edgar Degas recaptured in *Young Spartans Exercising*. Through his art, he questioned nineteenth-century views on class and gender. Women "wrestled" their way through history, in the works of Botticelli, Raphael and Rubens.

At Basic Inquiry, models stretch body and limb in dynamic poses: varied, twisted (contrapposto) and straight ahead (symmetric), all the while maintaining a steady neutral gaze.

What I have is an empathetic current
Recharging the insurgent
Breaking the tablets, like Moses.

Master draftsman Edgar Degas portrayed ballet dancers in pastels, bridging the gap between drawing and painting. Degas had to stop painting due to retinal disease. He turned to pastels, working in the controlled light of theatres or in his studio, away from the sun's glare.

Steve does the work indoors at Basic Inquiry with its overhead lighting. Most of the artists use sketch tools, but some integrate photography.

When Steve sees members' works of photography or digitalized art exhibited on the walls, he becomes more than a little annoyed. Like the Impressionists, who were very much against "the doctrine...

that the painter should be no more than a sensitive well-informed camera,"[60] Steve is of their school.

In a BBC television series John Berger talks about how "the photographer's way of seeing is reflected in his choice of subject. The painter's way of seeing is reconstituted by the marks he makes on the canvas or paper."[61]

Steve prickles at the idea of photography representing the art of the nude. He's an echo of French essayist Charles Baudelaire, who stated, "If photography is allowed to stand in for art...it will soon supplant or corrupt it completely."[62]

In a *Baltimore Sun* article, Glenn McNatt explains how photography first imitated painting. Painting then steered away from realism, only to borrow back some abstraction from what the camera could do.[63]

Steve has missed out on the technological advances of the 1980s and 1990s. Missing out is part of his gap. Bernie is a photographer/ manager at Basic. Steve likes Bernie's soft-spoken way of bouncing around ideas. Bernie updates him on photography, showing Steve his work.

I take snaps of Steve's work to email to family members every week. I am not using a computer or camera tool to represent or augment his work, only to communicate to others what he's doing.

Steve focuses on what Kenneth Clark[64] calls the energetic nude, in stark contrast with the nude of pathos, death and destruction.

I'm on the lookout for ways to frame Steve's energetic nudes. At first, the frames I find are inexpensive but damaged. They have chipped or broken glass or are difficult to unclip. Some have backings that are stuck to the matting or frame. Some have paper seals. Some are glued. Some have nails on the inside, making them difficult to un-sheathe. Enough. I hunt for frames in bulk at the art store, or on sale, to satisfy the prudent artiste.

I pry Steve's pieces away from him. I mat them and store them at home in the Corcoran Gallery. Adjacent to the laundry and furnace room, the space is an airy one where I pass from garage to upper level in our townhouse. The framed pieces are on the wall or leaning against it in boxes. The furnace whispers three times on the hour and sounds like Steve blowing pastel dust. I sit here, observing his work, crafting mine. Tolstoy captures the moment: "By words one transmits thoughts to another...by means of art, one transmits feelings."[65]

CHAPTER 7

Paint

STEVE IS COMING UNSTUCK—obsessing less. He is lighter. I like to think it has to do with how each drawing brings a kind of completion. Completion inspires change, which, according to *How You Can Help: A Toolkit for Families*,[66] comes in five stages: pre-contemplation, contemplation, preparation, action and maintenance.

Doing art has brought a lot of positive change into his life. Every week, we complete three sketches. We complete a shop and a visit—a special sibling achievement. But as the family toolkit suggests, problem solving also brings a waxing and waning of determination. On any given day, an art exhibit might seem worthwhile; the next, it's "a terrible idea, Joan." If it's up to me to motivate change with empathy and support, then I must avoid argument and roll with resistance.[67]

※

"Let's go to RONA, Joan. I need some paint," Steve says after a sketch session at Basic.

"What for?" I ask, but he doesn't specify.

Steve draws well, but he isn't a painter. Not in the artistic sense: not acrylic, not oil, not watercolour. Truth is, he has an aversion to artists' paint. Where latex and primer *wall* paint are concerned, though, it is love at first swipe.

Whenever I drop him and his groceries at the top step, I notice cans of it—stacked in the corner on the veranda, under plastic and paper bags and crushed cardboard boxes. Up the stairwell, the walls have roller marks of white paint applied in fan-like accordions. I'm reminded of a fictional character that does this with paint...one that Steve knows all too well.

Mild-mannered Mole pursues a spring-cleaning paint ritual in *The Wind in the Willows*. Steve tires of whitewashing like Mole, or so it appears from the stairwell's whitewash accordions. He has an illustrated hardcover copy that he lends me. He has no need for it. It's indelibly imprinted in his mind. Animated creatures come to life for Steve as audiovisual hallucinations.

Was it Mole who empowered Steve to come out of his hole for a while with me? (Mole, and Steve's other morphs—Bart, Clown, Bilbo—are his gang of good guys.) Steve doesn't tell me about them; he lends me the book. Occasionally, he impersonates characters, imitating perfectly the dialect, the lilt, the expression. He never says, "This one's my English accent; this one's my wise old man, my impish boy, or my clown," but I clue in.

Mole comes out of his hole to enjoy the nearby river with his sidekick, Ratty. Steve tunnels out of his hoard with me. Why? It could be as simple as: "Spring was moving in the air above and in the earth below and around him, penetrating even his dark and lowly little house with its spirit of divine discontent and longing."[68]

I'm a bit like Ratty, a creator of doggerel (poetry that's gone to the dogs) and lover of boats—in my case, the double kayak I share with Ken. Steve may recall that Ratty holds no sway on the mole hole. Neither do I hold sway on any household cleanup at Steve's (unless it's in a very early pre-contemplative stage).

"Why don't I take these old paint cans to recycling, Steve?"

"I'm in the middle of a tidy up," Steve says. "Leave it, Joan."

Splotches of whitewash smudge his black leather jacket, his hands, his shoes, his clothing. Whitewash is a poor man's paint, with antibacterial qualities. Carbon dioxide cures into calcium carbonate and makes it cooling and sanitizing for dairy barns and the bases of orchard trees. Does Steve know this about whitewash?

Mark Twain's Tom Sawyer character is tasked with whitewashing a fence. He ends up commandeering his friends to do the job for him. Such is his power of persuasion, a power to make others relish the dirty work: "The retired artist [Tom] sat on a barrel in the shade close by, dangled his legs, munched his apple, and planned the slaughter of more innocents."[69]

Steve doesn't coerce me into painting his hallway, but I'm at RONA, out of my depth. RONA has so many types and sizes and brands of paint, it's dizzying. There are pigments, additives, diluents, binders and resins, flat finish and semigloss, solvents and paint removers, indoor and outdoor paints.

There are paint additives with VOCs (volatile organic compounds) that vaporize at room temperature, and there are mould-resistant paints for kitchens and bathrooms. Steve's makeshift kitchen is part of his cramped area where he stores brushes, pans and cleanup guck, willy-nilly.

Thank goodness, he chooses not to add artists' paint to the disorder. Not that I've seen him limit disorder, but he limits his painting activity to that which goes on the wall, versus on a canvas. Whitewash is what he's after.

At RONA I don't see whitewash anywhere. Steve buys an equivalent of it, and he applies it with Mole- and Tom-Sawyer-like fervour.

The word whitewashing can also refer to psychological cleansing: an idiomatic expression for covering up sins, averting blame—a kind of absolution. Whitewashing is Steve's antidote to hoarding.

Buddhist nun Pema Chodron has said, "When we feel inadequate and unworthy, we hoard things….We hold on…to comfort ourselves…out of fear."[70]

I try my one-to-two-year rule on Steve: "Steve, if you haven't used it for two years, toss it. Better yet, recycle it."

"Easy for you, Joan," he says.

Hoarding disorder is consistent with schizophrenia's "disorganized thinking." My hoarder brother lays my two-year rule aside his ten-to-twenty-year rule and contemplates it. (Contemplation: an early stage of change.)

A poorly vented apartment is an unsafe storage space for paint products. Full stop. Darren and I know that Steve is familiar with wood stains and lacquers from his woodworking days. They, along with paint, are worrisome fire hazards.

Darren calls me. "Hey, I met up with Lawrence over lunch."

"Nice. How'd it go?"

"He wants Steve's space tidied up." (Lawrence insists upon this every year or so. We're thankful he's so lenient.)

"How are we going to do that?"

"Tell Steve we'll do an inspection next week."

"Great." I'm really not that excited about it.

I call Dr. P and he says, "Make it as surgical as possible."

It is my first time inside Steve's place. I've seen the cluttered stairs and the glassed-in veranda: the space he shares with Lawrence. While Darren talks to Steve downstairs, I head up with a broom and garbage bag. We have forewarned Steve of our "inspection."

I get to the top of the stairs and crab-walk into the main room. To the left, a hallway leads to what once was a bedroom, but both spaces are now crammed with stuff. When I drag open the twisted closet door, it is full of old hangers, but no clothing is hung. Clothing bits and pieces are littered, layered and lying around—on the floor, by the bed, draped. Piles of books, outdated magazines and journals are strewn so that no furniture is recognizable.

What is recognizable is the smell. Steve's smell. Steve doesn't have body odour; it is more a pungent gritty smell, mixed with a white powder he sprinkles the way Peter Pan sprinkles pixie dust from Tinker Bell onto his flying protege, Wendy.

White sediment frosts the floor, and I imagine Steve twirling and sprinkling, the residue landing on the floor and on him. Him, flying around the room. Instead of hoovering dirt into a vacuum bag, Steve expels powder.

To the right off the landing, Steve's bathtub is full of old yogurt containers and dishes, roller pans, bits of paintbrushes, bits of rags, bits of bits, and worst of all, it is mucky. Bathing, if it ever happens, would entail sink sponge baths.

"What about one of those bathtub refits, Steve? They come in and custom line the tub with a bath fitter...in and out in one day."

"No thank you, Florence. No thank you, Nancy Drew," he says.

I fall, in Steve's estimation, somewhere between Nurse Florence Nightingale, a nineteenth-century reformer, and Nancy Drew, fictional girl detective, when I try to intervene or step beyond my role as art manager into the realm of health-and-hoarding sleuth.

I can't tackle Steve's mess. I don't know where to begin. Darren tells me how he got his daughter to clean up her room by bringing her to Steve's.

All I can handle is the art, some errands and a bit o' bocce, I think.

The rest is as overpowering as the smell that permeates his books and bags. Grime, his residue. Grime, his cologne.

I sweep haphazardly and put empty pizza boxes in the garbage bag.

"What are you doing?" Steve has come upstairs and is looking at me with dismay.

"Just cleaning up a bit, Steve. The pizza box smell might attract rats."

"The only rats I smell are you and Darren. Quit it," he says.

"Steve," says Darren, who's followed him upstairs, "we'll give you two months to toss some of this junk. We'll be back with a dumpster."

"Harrumph," says Steve.

"Well, we tried," I say to Darren in the car.

"Just call me Dumpster Darren," Darren says.

※

In early episodes of the *Peanuts* comic strip, Pigpen was a dirt dignitary who said, "I haven't got a name...people just call me things...real insulting things."[71] In later episodes, Charles M. Schultz, the creator, wrote Pigpen out of the series. Turns out dirt jokes aren't all that funny.

A new member at a Basic Inquiry session says, "Your brother is so smelly and dirty."

"Do you think you can sit somewhere else? Because there's not much I can do about it," I reply.

She doesn't come back. For the most part, I'm indebted to Basic members for their tolerance.

In an attempt at cleanliness, I introduce Steve to the local laundromat; we go there twice, but he can't organize the steps involved, even with the bicycle panniers I get him. I wash a garbage bag full of dirty clothes every other week.

"Steve, let me have that jacket; it's gross." (It is the jacket I gave him for Christmas, and he loves its bagginess—its zips, snaps and Velcro pocket flaps.)

"Don't bother, Joan," he says. (My parents used to say that.)

"Slip it in here and I'll have it back to you next week," I say.

He gives it to me. Or to be more exact, he lets me take it.

※

Away from the chaos, Steve takes the beginner and intermediate painting classes at the Art Studios with Bev and Julian, without me.

Both facilitators are qualified artists, and I'm hoping he'll enjoy this new art medium.

"Joan, maybe Steve could try a class on his own," says Ann.

"I'm totally fine with that," I say. And I am. I don't want to baby (or, as Darren suggested, babysit) Steve. And I also think he has room for art more than one day a week at Basic. That is not to be.

I purchase some acrylics from a paint supply list that Bev gives me, and I sign myself up for a series of classes, in case Steve takes to it like I am. My class consists of ten night-school classes to complete an acrylic still life from a photograph. My favourite is a vase of flowers on a window ledge. What fifteen people turn out fascinates me: all as different as what writers do when prompted on the same topic.

I try a Saturday afternoon acrylics session with a local landscape painter, Maria Josenhans. Maria takes us through the steps in *plein-air* painting. It is complementary to writing, this artful study. I appreciate the building blocks of compositional painting. I'm pleased enough with the result to prop one on my living room window ledge.

Similarities exist between writing and painting—both art forms establish a point of view or an angle; both start with a quick sketch to determine what to include and what to leave out; both fill in and blot out until a picture or idea takes shape.

I buy a full spectrum of 150-millilitre tubes of Stevenson Acrylics, noting the irony of Steve's name in the brand. I also buy us each a set of not-quite-top-dollar brushes in a variety of sizes, and two rubber hand-held spatula applicators, just for fun. Brush cleaner and a butcher tray for mixing palette colours top off the list.

I love learning about colour: the primary and complementary, the warm and the cool. Acrylics dry quickly; Steve could do one or two per session at Basic, but no. He sticks with pastel, except for one or two experiments.

I tuck several paint tubes into our toolkit. Basic Inquiry sessions are full of artistic peers, each doing their own thing in a variety of ways. Steve grabs a paint tube from the supply box on the floor between us. I take note, but it's not just any tube. Stevenson Titanium White. Squeezing it like toothpaste, Steve uses the rubber applicator to spread it on his mixed-media-and-pastel piece. It covers smudge marks. It makes the image pop.

※

A contour blade is a rubber, hand-held tool for spreading paint. We leave the brushes unused. The blade is as effective as charcoal outlines in delineating and accentuating the figure. Steve blades white paint onto big pieces of cardboard as a finishing touch; pastel paper hasn't got the teeth to hold paint.

Just like the 1960s Colgate toothpaste ad—I guess we are "a one-toothpaste family again."[72]

Like the whitewash in his stairwell and the white dust on his floor, blades of whiteness freshen the work.

※

Jackson Pollock was an abstract expressionist of the 1940s and 1950s who dripped and splattered his way to fame on huge canvases. He didn't use brushes, but instead poured paint using knives, trowels and sticks to shape the free form. Steve would have heard of him in his art school days. Steve tries a Jackson Pollock experiment that backfires a bit. But that's just my take. Artists don't make mistakes.

Steve drips red, dark blue and lime green paint over an orange wash. It's the first thing he's completed at home (probably in the yard or on the exterior back stairs). He lets the poster board dry and tells me to collage some of his pastel figures overtop. They aren't really splatters; they are blobs. They look planetary—solar system-like. I cut out figures from rolls of sketch paper where Steve's figures are strong, but the backgrounds are spoiled. Juxtaposed over his splattered background, one figure reminds me of fictional superhero Wonder Woman. She's actually a he, as I remember the powerful model, but no matter. "They" are a trio of figure collages that could be panelled and hinged together like modern photographic triptyches.

When Dr. P's office is looking to put art on the mental health unit walls, I carry the three pieces, framed and ready, to one of Steve's appointments. Dr. P is encouraging. But there seems to be a catch. The mental health office's suicide-prevention program doesn't like the drips of red. They call to tell me.

"I'm the one who taped the figures over the splatter," I explain. "It wasn't Steve's idea." Steve hasn't juxtaposed the figures over the painted backgrounds. Still, they reject them because the red suggests blood. I'm not sure how to tell Steve. Statistics show that as many as 60 percent of males with schizophrenia attempt suicide, with 10 to 15 percent being successful. I don't know if he has ever considered it, but most attempts are in the period of early diagnosis, or in an active phase of the illness. By now, Steve has had schizophrenia for over thirty-five years.

We take the framed pieces home with us. In the meantime, I mention the conundrum to Ann Webborn. Ann works not only at the Art Studios, but also for the South Mental Health team.

She says, "Our mental health unit would be delighted to exhibit Steve's splatter-paint collages."

The following week, I tell Steve. "Steve, Ann, from the Art Studios, also works at a mental health unit. They want to display your pieces."

"I thought we were putting them on Dr. P's wall," says Steve.

"Yes, but they have a problem with it." I want to gloss over it.

"Oh?" He is waiting for my response.

"Their suicide-prevention team thinks the red splatter looks like blood." There. I've said it. Steve is as nonchalant as if I just told him the time.

We visit Ann at her mental health workplace and drop off the pieces; they find a home.

The backfire rebounds to become an outcome worthy of artistic examination—a playful element of creativity.

※

One day when we are leaving Basic, Steve says, "The rule today is no talking."

"Uh-huh," I nod dumbly.

"Drive to the pickup area of the Salvation Army, Joan."

"Uh…" I am happy we aren't going to RONA for more paint.

"Don't say anything," Steve says. I nod.

Steve gets out of the car and goes in, and the two employees roll an oven into the loading bay. I back up the car as directed, and they load it into my utility vehicle. It is a perfect fit. We drive to Steve's. The whole while I am thinking: *How are we going to get this monolith inside? How can I, a double hip replacement who's not supposed to do heavy lifting, possibly help him?*

"My old oven is crap," Steve says.

"Wait here," he says as we park outside his home.

I wait. I'm learning to wait.

He comes back with a roll of old carpeting and some heavy-duty plastic. He tips the oven out of the car onto the narrow grass boulevard. Using the plastic and the carpet roll, he drags the oven to the foot of the exterior stairs.

What now? I think.

But he says, "I'll take the weight. You support it."

He coaxes the oven, and me, up the stairs. He has leeway…about six feet, tipping and rocking. Once at the top, we squeeze through the two front doors, and at the foot of the interior staircase, he has half the jimmy room.

"I've got it, Joan. You steady it," he says. There is a weight between us. I am above him, with its bulk blocking my view of him, but I can hear him. He is working hard, panting. I know it is heavy. We stop halfway up the stairs. Each step is a grunt. He is Atlas with the weight of the world on his shoulders.

"Take it easy, Steve; it's not worth hurting yourself."

Halfway up the stairs, there is no going back...if we are going to make it. Could we break the side window? Could the oven fall on him? Could one or both of us get injured? Possibly all of the above.

But it unfolds just as he's planned. He manoeuvres it each step of the way. With a bit of support, he makes it work. At the top landing, Steve says, "Okay. I'll take it from here."

How is he going to carve a path to where he wants it through all the junk? How is he going to get rid of the old one? Is it electrically compatible? A safe hookup?

I am learning to execute tasks as requested—to stand back and respect his way of doing things.

More than any of these considerations is the illness itself. It is the weight that he carries.

Make it lighter. That's my job. He continues to figure out ways to manage, to cope. And of course there is our date with Darren and the dumpster.

By the time that happens a month later, he and Darren have an old oven to dispose of. I fill a few bags with loose paper (and the familiar pizza boxes), sweep up and sanitize the bathroom. They drag the old oven to Steve's tiny, north-facing balcony and tip it into the yard. It lands with a thud on the soft grass. The dumpster is only half full. It is enough to satisfy the landlord.

"We've left some room for your stuff, Lawrence," we say. Lawrence smiles.

I leave liquid soap and baking soda behind for Steve. Baking soda is my favourite multi-purpose cleaning powder. It's white, so maybe Steve will like it. Odourless. I tell him how I sprinkle it on a soapy, wet J-Cloth to clean the sink and the tub. Then scrub-a-dub-dub.

The three of us celebrate over coffee at a local café. We've put more than a dint in the yard. We've put a dint in the process of change.

※

Here's my tribute to Steve, written in the two-thousand-year-old, four-line style of Qu Yuan:

Listen to the wetness roll up the wall
In overlapping strokes
Smoothing smudges
Like a new tide.

CHAPTER 8

Fixative

AT STEVE'S FIRST ART EXHIBIT, *Dancing on the Interface*, six of his fifty-seven pieces sell. We sell cards with his images, too. Steve doesn't come to the opening. I suppose chit-chat might lead to mental turmoil. He doesn't explain, nor does he need to. I want him to know that I am proud. Of him. So there.

On the day of the opening, it is a rare snowstorm in Vancouver. Adam, at the Safari Café next door to Basic, caters the food, which, although plentiful and beautifully presented, attracts few attendees. Members come to openings for the party atmosphere to support the social bonds that Steve does not have. They don't necessarily buy each other's art (some have told me they barely have wall space for their own). It's up to the artist-exhibitors to invite outsiders, but in this case, this manager extends an invitation to a smattering of artists, family and friends.

Steve's art will be in the gallery/studio for a month. We'll look at it for the next four Tuesdays, plus private exhibit times that I've agreed to sit in on. Success, by my definition, is satisfied in this achievement of exhibiting. Steve doesn't bother with any concept of success.

Nonetheless, he has become an artist-exhibitor. The weather hasn't let us down; it has let everyone off the hook.

I put an artist's biography on the wall in its own frame; it reads: "Panel #1 entitled *Alice*—(Steve) began a journey back to *Basics* and down the creative rabbit hole some six years ago."

Alice, a mature member and potter at the Art Studios, had done a sitting for Steve at an Art Studios sketch class; he signed, dated and named the sketch *Alice*. He rarely does all three nowadays: sign, date and title, although dating practice pieces with an ink stamp does happen from time to time.

Alice conveys, as Steve's sketches continue to do, "the surveyor and the surveyed...a sense of being appreciated as herself by another."[73] Two sketchers at their easels are in the grey background, outlined in burnt-orange Conté crayon. Alice is in a dress, etched in charcoal, with skin-tone blush on her face and legs, sitting snugly in her white sweater, hands folded in her lap.

In the work, the surveyed figure is drawn realistically, while the surveyors are caricatured. Steve knew that Alice, who was older than him, still cranked out Art—in that never-too-late way. Steve's portrayal of Alice was far from perfect. He drew her right arm twice, like a third limb, camouflaging it into her skirt as if she was moulding herself from a potter's wheel—the stool on which she sat. Her sweater's textural swirls were flurries of white correction fluid. It marked his beginning with drawn figures.

The bio continues: "Steve funnels his skill and energy into the portraits and figures you see around you. Some are collaged. Many include a backdrop of easels and people. Steve has been a welder/woodworker. He attended the Vancouver School of Art in the 1970s. Virtually self-taught, in this body of work, 2006 to 2011, his pastel figures are in dialogue with one another.

"Please sign the guest book to relay your feedback. Steve sends his best regards for a fun evening. Tip a glass, visit and *Dance on the Interface*."

Shelley Rothenburger, MFA, a member and model at Basic Inquiry Studio and Gallery, encourages Steve to put up the show. She isn't tentative with her praise. Shelley's comment in the guest book reads: "His work is like a combination of Picasso, Cezanne and the German Expressionists with a little Matisse on the side. Picasso with bold line and shape, Cezanne with strong forms and composition, German Expressionist with the rawness of emotion and technique, and Matisse with the one dancing figure piece and strong collages."

What Shelley has said is important to me, and I think Steve appreciates it too. For me, it is concise and colossal. There is a universe within it. She is an art educator, attributing what she sees with what she knows. Shelley sees the layers and the influences. Delving into past artists' lives, and the movements they initiated, helps me appreciate and understand Steve's work moving forward and, later, put it in perspective.

Matisse was wheelchair-bound and in ill health when he began using collage (from the French *coller*, "to glue") and decoupage (French for "to cut out"). Scissors became his shaping tools in *Blue Nude II*.

Cézanne made a connection between Impressionism and Cubism with works such as *Large Bathers*. He stretched his work into Post-Impressionism with colour, shape and multiple viewpoints in works such as *The Boy in the Red Vest*.

The German Expressionist Franz Marc did *Yellow Cow* and *Blue Horse*, two separate paintings, which suggest the raw emotion and technique that Shelley refers to. (Animal subjects also constitute life or figure drawing.) The primary colours Franz Marc used were representative of male (blue) and female (yellow) energy. Some say his *Blue Horse* was a self-portrait.

Nudes and semi-clad models are portrayed throughout art history in romanticized, naturalistic and realistic settings: boudoir to bordello, ballet bar to wrestling ring to picnic-blanketed riverside.

Since prehistory, Venus statuettes—faceless, with pendulous breasts and wide hips—have depicted the desire, purity and emotion of residing in the flesh. Nudity reminds us of our origins in creative freedom, without barriers. We stop hiding. We remove layers. We reveal ourselves.

Artists show the way, and in so doing, they become freer. This is a genre of art that's working for Steve. I enjoy witnessing his new-found freedom.

Shelley's admiration of Steve's work seems to be catching on. Elizabeth, Margaret and Sim help hang the show. They like what Steve is doing. What he and I are doing together ripples outward to an artistic family.

In three to four hours, we hang the fifty-seven pieces. Elizabeth is experienced in hanging shows; she leads us. We take each piece out of its box and lean it against the wall, box-buffered. We group the pieces by colour, by landscape or portrait orientation (most of Steve's are in portrait orientation) and by intuition. Before measuring, marking and hanging, we number them one to fifty-seven.

From his woodwork and welding days, Steve brings grain and structure to his sketches. Fellow artists enjoy "the bright, open palette, the free lines, the expressionistic qualities" and "how the dancing pastels maintain a precarious balance." These skilled observers put these remarks in the guest book.

Sandra Yuen MacKay is an artist and author[74] that Steve and I met at the Art Studios. She attends *Dancing on the Interface* in February of 2011. "I was struck by the vigorous strokes, colour and abstract qualities of the works," Sandra writes.

I tell Nick, one of the regular attendees at Basic Inquiry, how I love Sandra's comment, since artists help me define what I'm seeing in Steve's work. Next thing I know, Nick is scribbling thoughtfully into the book: "Beautiful shapes, but what I love about seeing them all together is watching the black line snake from inner anatomy to outer calligraphy, across the canvasses."

Certainly Steve's charcoal lassoes and corrals his reality. He's a mixed-media cowboy.

Sculptural qualities blend form and figure in Cézanne's *Three Bathers*, a painting Matisse owned all his artistic life, about which he said, "Fit your parts into one another...build up your figure as a carpenter does a house."

As a former woodworker, especially fond of burls, Steve is renovating his own artful house.

I'm making sense of it.

Make-Sense Sestina I

I never knew who you were talking to.
Yet Irish bards seem to know—
Shamans, with intuitive brains—
With eyesight fading—
Glaucoma needs no hint
For stigmatism to abound.

※

Greeks tagged verbs with the suffix *isma*, and in so doing, created action nouns (like *ing* gerunds in English: *portraying, sketching, drawing*), so that the practice of impressing (to affect deeply or make an influence) became Impressionism.

Author Bob Raczka[75] explains "isms"—the tag of many an art movement. He highlights Impressionism's effect of light on colour, which Cézanne and his mentor, Pissarro, portrayed. Steve dabs some of that -ism onto his work with looseness and colour. Manet and Matisse also used black for their shadows, whereas other Impressionists depicted shadow-shading in blue or purple.

It takes an -ism noun to fly like a verb. It takes a brother like Steve to lift his artful wings.

In Fauvism, Matisse expressed emotion in quick, bold colours, which gave some of his works a sketchy, unfinished look. Fauvism quickly made way for Expressionism, with its feeling-over-thought spontaneity and quick, aggressive lines. Steve borrows from that -ism too.

In Abstract Expressionism, Jackson Pollock dripped paint with an active physicality. He and Steve are independent loners, outliers, such as the people that author Malcolm Gladwell spoke of: "I'm interested in people who are outliers—in men and women who, for one reason or another, are so accomplished and so extraordinary and so outside of ordinary experience….It's those who lie outside ordinary experience who have the most to teach us."[76]

Steve's pieces are teaching me the value of self-expression. He captures a wedge of -ism, that wedge of active practice, in all his pieces. I wish I could relay which ones, and name the titles of those pieces, but he doesn't title his pieces.

Ann Webborn comes to the show, and I ask her what to do about his anonymity. "Never mind," she says. "Let the pieces speak for themselves."

※

Make-Sense Sestina II

Disorder leapt, out of bounds—
In piles of clothes & paint cans, too
That kept me out; gave you a hint—
An idea of how to know
When antagonism was fading—
Healing fragmented brains.

※

But I do mind. I try to persuade Steve to sign and title his pieces, but he won't. I try to get him to agree to a value, but he won't. I may be his manager, but I'm not qualified to name or sign his work. How to know when a piece is finished, and who am I to say? How do I judge quality or worth? What is truly great art? I number them instead, and Basic artists say, "I like #34 for its energy and colour." Or "My favourite is #25, lovely composition." Or "I dig the vigour and energy of these expressionistic pieces—great colour! I enjoyed #24 and #17 especially."

Steve asks me, "Do you think Vincent van Gogh would be famous today?" He has doubts he won't expand upon.

Like Theo van Gogh, Vincent's art-dealer brother, I am the younger, admiring sibling. After Theo's death (six months after Vincent's), Theo's widow, Johanna van Gogh-Bonger, took over the Van Gogh collection. Everyone did not share her enthusiasm. Richard Roland Holst stated:

"Mrs. Van Gogh is a charming little woman, but it irritates me when someone gushes fanatically on a subject she knows nothing about, and although blinded by sentimentality still thinks she is adopting a strictly critical attitude....The work that Mrs. Van Gogh would like best is the one that was the most bombastic and sentimental, the one that made her shed the most tears."[77]

Basic Inquiry members suggest prices for their artwork. I listen to other estimates and smack a figure on Steve's works. I try not to gush. Asking a little less for an unframed piece saves me unfettering fourteen quick-release frames.

As far as fettering goes, I buy in bulk: fifty 18-by-24-inch aluminum frames at Opus Art Supplies. They are contained in shipping boxes with glass, an acid-free backing barrier, hanging clips, plastic-coated wire and, alas, multiple quick releases. Since I am still learning, each piece takes me more than one go to frame. For the sake of approximation, two goes multiplied by fifty frames.

I remove the quick releases, tape the art in and pop the releases back. Thousands of thumb push-ups later, we have one show, plus or minus another thousand, for the ones I notice are crooked and have to redo. Double-sided tape holds them in place inside the frame. For most pieces, Steve spends forty-five minutes to an hour doing them at Basic Inquiry. His energy funnels like a stream of light through a magnifying glass. Steve's life experiences and creativity weld together.

※

Make-Sense Sestina III

For all the anger, disturb reigns—
Loss & paranoia know no bounds
In illogical speech. Far from fading,
You find your vital clue to
Configure & compose—No
Time for a model hint.

※

As a child, Steve was a nature boy, collecting and looking at bugs in jars through a magnifying glass. The magnifier localizes photons through a pinpoint. The sun's rays pass through and ignite kindling, such as newspaper, and possibly the bug that's resting on it. Now, Steve is the one on fire with his art. I am as ignitable as kindling, which is why untitled artwork burns me up. After a day of futile persuasion and the show's imminent opening, Steve is getting out of the car. We are done for the day. I pull over on Main Street to let him walk the short distance home.

"See you next week, Steve," I say.

"You don't like me very much do you?" he asks.

The passenger door is closing in my face. "No, Steve, I don't like you. I love you."

He looks at me. And there is a small smile on his face as he trundles off. Mine too.

※

Make-Sense Sestina IV

No time to pick up the hint
Of common-sense brains—
Expressionistic kernels you did know
Through handpicked tools—seeds abound—
Studying the line; the shade, to
Trowel the din within. Fading.

※

Wassily Kandinsky (1866–1944) is considered the Father of Abstract Art and was part of the age of Expressionism. His take? "I value only those artists who really are artists, that is, who consciously or unconsciously, in an entirely original form, embody the expression of their inner life; who work only for this end and cannot work otherwise,"[78] he said.

Steve is intent on the lofty goal of self-expressionism, which may extend to soul expressionism. Artistic lines snake through history. Did he study Kandinsky? They are united in the craft of doing: the art of manifesting expression.

"And what is that?" I've often asked myself. "And how does Steve define it in his work?"

Like most artists, he doesn't consciously insert his feelings into his art. Steve doesn't compose his figures. The models are there on the dais, for all to see. It must be that his emotional input is elemental in the line, colour, shape, space and form—and how they come together. Fluidly.

Figurative drawing lends itself to curved lines, which can bring comfort and ease, as much to the viewer as to the practitioner. And with sticks of charcoal, Conté and pastel, Steve applies thick lines, enhancing and reinforcing his ease in his own natural strength. He values tone; he lavishes in it. He lavishes it on.

Some have told me they feel an overwhelming emotion looking at the body of Steve's work. In the myriad of emotions—up to thirty-four thousand, by some estimates—Dr. Robert Plutchik, an American psychologist, has narrowed it down to four opposing pairs: joy and sadness, anger and fear, trust and distrust, and surprise and anticipation, and like the colour wheel, they blend into one another in countless hues.[79]

I suppose I should have asked the Basic artists, "What is it that touches you?" But one theory (of mine) is that Steve is dispelling the negative emotions of sadness, fear and distrust and is learning to embrace joy. He's trusting in an element of joyful surprise (with the odd flare-up of anger, an emotion often considered more positive than fear).

Many of his portraits show a left-cheek bias,[80] showing off the more expressive (and attractive) left profile. How many actors and politicians stall photo ops with, "Wait. Make sure you get my good side"? They inevitably mean their left side. Artists favour the left side's expressiveness.

I submit his work to the Art Rental Programme, North Vancouver Community Arts Council (now known as North Van Arts) at CityScape Gallery, whose staff jury art twice a year. I enter three pieces at a time; I drop them off in the morning and go back later to see which of the three are accepted. Two are typically chosen to hang on the art rental racks. Those pieces that sell help pay for more art supplies and frames. I sell another half-dozen.

We also exhibit at a Main Street coffee shop, the Grind & Gallery Coffee Bar. I'm putting up Steve's exhibit posters when we find it. Walking up Main, Ken and I have been sleuthing for bulletin boards or shops amenable to posters. We walk in; it looks small.

"Okay if I leave a poster about an art exhibit?" I ask.

"Bulletin board's in the back," the server says.

The tiny space magnifies tenfold, with art on the walls. Proprietors Michelle and Jay welcome artists' exhibits.

I drop by the coffee shop with Steve, once his work is hung. He is restless and wants to get home, so we are there all of five minutes. I can't entice him to stay, even for a coffee to admire his work. He's out the door. When not doing art, he's a rambling man, mentally and physically.

"Is that your brother?" asks Michelle.

"Yes. Does that surprise you?" I say.

"Only that he's created works of such beauty," she replies.

Maybe that's the emotive quality Steve is uncovering.

※

Make-Sense Sestina V

The dis-, the mis-, the il-, the in- are fading:
The unreal and irrelevant hint
Undoes the glue to
Reduce delusional brains
To precious abounds,
The way well water is drawn & known.

※

Grind Writers meet at the Gallery Coffee Bar every two weeks. I see their poster. I join them. I enjoy scratching the writing surface with the group's founder and facilitator, Margo Lamont.

I've installed thirty-two of Steve's fifty-seven pieces there with Ken's help. Because the coffee shop is open to the public (and families and children), they allow the impressionistic nude pieces only if the nudity isn't explicit. One Saturday morning, the writers let the pieces guide our prompt. (Ann's comment on letting them speak for themselves prompted *me*.) Prompts are ideas, suggestions, topics, short phrases or...pictures that churn the writing juices.

There are thirty-two pieces hung on the walls in the back room's windowless space. The Grind Writers push three or four tables together at the back, up two steps above the patrons' working laptops. About six of Steve's pieces surround our table, but my view falls on a head-and-shoulders shot he did of a model, in two perspectives. She looks straight out at the viewer, and she also looks sideways, as if whispering in her double's ear.

She reminds me of my initial awkwardness with nudes as an art form. I create a dialogue between two fictional friends; I call it "Less Isn't More." What more or less becomes apparent is that I've begun stripping away my own layers.

I have a secret, says my fictional self. (Let's call her Gloria.)

We don't have secrets...well, not since grade two, says my confidante, Sylvia.

Something to tell you, Gloria presses.

Okay, okay...do tell.

I've got a new job, Gloria says.

Well, fantastic! What's the big deal? asks Sylvia.

You might wonder, Gloria says.

What do you mean?

I'm modelling, Sylvia. (I'm modelling for Steve; he is modelling for me; we are modelling for each other. Modelling as showing, imitating and representing.)

Models make great money, Gloria. What? Designer clothes, lingerie? asks Sylvia.

Less, Sylvia.

Less what, money? she asks.

The rule of less, Gloria says.

What's that? asks Sylvia.

The less you wear, the more you make.

Don't you make more money wearing less?

No, Gloria says.

Why not? asks Sylvia.

Because I wear nothing...except maybe a scarf, says Gloria.

How does that work? she asks.

Well, I show up for work, says Gloria.

Where?

At a life-drawing studio, says Gloria.

Who's there...do they watch? Sylvia is starting to enjoy herself.

The artists sit around me. I'm on a small, raised platform, Gloria says.

Do they play burlesque music? Sylvia asks.

No! says Gloria.

What about between poses? Sylvia asks.

I put on a robe, Gloria says.

How long's the session?

At first they're short—three-, five- and ten-minute poses up to thirty minutes, replies Gloria.

Do you move around? Show me one of your poses, says Sylvia.

No, you commit to one pose, says Gloria.

Come on; let's see one, says Sylvia.

Ta-da!

Does your "hoohoo" ever show? Sylvia asks.

Look, my hoohoo is not an issue, says Gloria.

Since when? asks Sylvia.

Hoohoos aren't key. This isn't porn, Gloria says.

Do you get to look at their work? she asks.

At the break, I circulate, Gloria replies.

Respectful? she asks.

Absolutely...one guy even gave me his half-hour sketch, says Gloria.

(I've practiced Iyengar yoga long enough to know holding poses takes stamina—the downward-facing dog, the plank, the shoulder stand and headstand are poses I hold for one minute, maximum.)

You choose the pose carefully. I've seen shaking limbs. Models cramp up.

I don't think I could hold that for thirty minutes, says Sylvia.
Never know till you try.
Not on your life! she says.
Well, it isn't called life drawing for nothing. Gloria is a master of the one-liner, like Steve and me.

※

Life drawing is making an impression on me. I am that dubious friend who couldn't graduate from *Drawing on the Right Side of the Brain* classes to life-drawing sessions. I never model. Neither does Steve. Not in that way, shape or form.

Philosopher and writer Roman Krznaric[81] refers to a shift in mental framework that helps make an imaginative yet empathetic leap into Steve's shoes, like the one I experienced with the oven transfer. More understanding helps guide and promote empathy's actions.

I'm getting a fix on it—securing an attachment.

※

Fixative is essentially hairspray without perfume. It is to pastels what varnish is to wood. It sticks the chalky grains of pastel together, holds them in position and prevents smudging. Steve prefers dollar-store hairspray to fixative. It costs less. A bit like he is with paint, Steve is oblivious to the toxic quality of additives. I buy the art store's unadulterated fixative and lightly spray his sketches, outside in the fresh air.

To fix is to stabilize or set into focus. I'd like to advocate a fix for Steve—not a quick fix, more of a reset button. Dad did that as a wartime air observer/navigator, fixing locations for the B-24 Liberators in which he flew. If I could be that kind of fixer-observer, helping to steer a course, I might help liberate Steve. In so doing, I might liberate myself.

Make-Sense Sestina VI

& so, no need to know—
Of the waning: the fading
When colourful splashes & black outlines abound—
A serene & sure hint
That consolidated our brains—
To complete the whole—we two.

Pollock, Matisse & Van Gogh did know the telling hint

Of fading line, colour & space engrained—

That resound dimensionally like an old tattoo.

CHAPTER 9

Stump

WHO SEES DEATH coming?

After the late winter exhibit of 2011, many changes were coming for me, although Steve and I continued our Tuesday routine into 2012.

I delve into my calendar and journals from the time and see how time evaporated. I retired from teaching that spring. Ken and I flew to Panama and took a two-week bus trip through its canal and locks. I joined writing workshops, a local writing association (North Shore Writers) and a book club. Over the course of a year, I set up a blog and a website, and I posted poetic YouTube videos, mostly environmental in nature. I journalled, blogged and had my first travel adventure published.

Steve's pieces were on display at the North Vancouver Community Arts Council Art Rental Programme. Basic Inquiry had more Member Shows. Steve's art was featured in their fundraising calendar. As 2013 approached, I considered whether a second exhibit might be a good goal for Steve. I started scooping pieces for the show, which I booked six months in advance, for the fall of 2013.

///

When we played bocce early in the summer of 2013, in our bent-bocce way, it was amblyopic eyesight or "lazy eye" that waggled its befuddling finger, saying, "Move over, myopia."

"Move the jack, Joan," Steve said. "I can't see it."

The white marker ball would slip into a hollow with only a little of its bald pate exposed. I could see it, but Steve couldn't, so we used shiny markers to prop it up, until I simply stood there as a target.

Steve, at long last, agreed to get his eyes checked. His right eye was 20/70, nearsighted, with astigmatism's out-of-focus blur. At twenty feet from an eye chart, 20/70 vision is what someone with normal vision (20/20) sees at seventy feet. Anything over 20/60 is visually impaired. Without a single point of reference in the retina, light scatters. Fuzziness follows.

Eyesight issues were almost as baffling to me as Steve's schizophrenia. I wear reading glasses (ones that magnify), yet his way of seeing was a combination of chronic mental illness, visual impairment and unique creativity. He picked up pieces of glass wherever he found them—clear prescriptive shards and coloured glass—and peered through them.

Had Steve's vision worsened from when we started doing art? I suppose it eroded over the decade. Basic Inquiry models were consistently twenty feet away. Steve's portraits depicted classic Renaissance faces—or was it something else altogether?

The North Vancouver Community Arts Council director said, "That's you, Joan."

"What do you mean?" I was stumped.

"Steve's sketching you. You are always the face closest to him. It looks like you."

I was not convinced. Of course I knew my image from photographs. But in a sketch, I wasn't sure whether I recognized myself.

In the portrait she was referring to, I tried to remember who the model had been that day. Did I, as was sometimes the case, get off my bench to sit on the floor, closer to the model? Or was I closer to Steve? Steve moved from time to time, but only around the circle, never closer to the model. I was portable. He, portly with his multiple layers of clothing and pockets full of treasure, didn't move as much.

He knew the symmetry of a face: the interplay of angles and shapes; the dance of energy required to get it right (it is arguably the easiest genre to get wrong); the circular cranium, the ovular head, the forehead, the jawline; the halfway placement of the eyes, the central nose, the mouth and chin; the hairline and ears.

Steve captured spatially seen 3-D models onto 2-D paper and froze them there . As both viewer and loving creator, he captured the close-up, yet still gave the viewer (and himself) space to ponder.

Did he sneak glances my way to verify what he couldn't see? The only thing that I was certain about was his deteriorating eyesight. In his final weeks, leading up to that eye exam, he got a visual acuity score of 20/200, with early cataracts in both eyes. His vision had been uncorrected since his twenties. He was legally blind in the left eye.

Steve had the Nicolaides book *The Natural Way to Draw*, in which he'd underlined the following: "Drawing depends on seeing. Seeing depends on knowing....To what the eye can see the artist adds feeling and thought. He can, if he wishes, relate for us the adventures of his soul in the midst of life."[82]

There was a transition going on for Steve, toward greater vision. I was the one who was blind to his broader health issues.

※

After that Oakridge Optometry clinical assessment, I put an order in to LensCrafters. These were two shopfronts we walked by most

Tuesdays at the Oakridge Centre mall. We rarely bumped into anyone we knew, but that day at the eye clinic, ninety-year-old Mrs. S sat there waiting for corrective lenses. Mrs. S came from the church of our youth, and her husband, Dr. S, had been our family physician. She looked as well-preserved to me as she had when I was eighteen, in an old-fashioned way, with her beige suit, handbag and hair just so.

"Hello Mrs. S," I said. "We're Corcorans: Joan and Steve. You knew our parents, Bert and Trudy, from St. John the Apostle Church."

"Oh, yes, I remember," she said. She talked about her husband and his heart problems, and his surgery that was "to do or die for." He did the latter. She said it matter of factly, the way a ninety-year-old can. And there was something soothing about that conversation with Mrs. S—her pointing the way along the road to the dark door that Mary Oliver wrote about in her poem, "When Death Comes":

When death comes
like the hungry bear in autumn...
I want to step through that door full of curiosity, wondering:
what is it going to be like, that cottage of darkness?

And therefore I look upon everything
as a brotherhood and a sisterhood
and I look upon time as no more than an idea[83]

But still, I didn't suspect Death, even when Steve hesitated on his top step, picked up the newspaper and, pointing to the obituaries, commented, "All these people battled cancer and lost." I remembered that comment later on, when I realized Steve knew he had a mass growing beneath his left rib cage.

Healthwise, in the past two years, he'd had extensive dental work as well as an infection in his foot from *blindly* stepping on a nail. That had required a tetanus shot.

"I'm being attacked by pinworms," he started saying in the fall of 2012. He didn't say anything about indigestion pain, diarrhea or nausea: signs that might have triggered my remembrance of Ken's early colon-cancer indicators.

A pinworm is a tapeworm—one of the most common intestinal infections in the world. Some people get tapeworms from under-cooked beef or pork. Steve's psychiatrist said it was unlikely that he had a parasite. Steve had been so strong and resilient to every-thing; I didn't suspect anything. I wasn't sure what to make of the pinworm notion.

"Steve, are you getting checkups from the medical clinic?" I asked.

"Yes, Florence," he assured me.

"Good to have a baseline," I said.

A few weeks later, after lunch and bocce, he vomited into the gutter before getting out of the car. "Better now," he said. Nothing more.

A touch of flu? I wondered.

Some weeks later, he did it again. "My mouth has become my anus," he said.

He gave the impression of someone viewing himself as an art instalment, coming apart piece by piece. Undoing his very self.

By August, we saw the new GP, who asked, "How many times have you vomited in the past month, Steve?"

He answered without hesitation, "Six times." He'd been keeping count.

※

He wanted a general practitioner once his psychiatrist retired, and Dr. P was ready to retire. Steve and Dr. P had met monthly for over twenty-five years. They shook hands and parted ways. Steve wanted annual checkups as opposed to monthly ones. It's not uncommon for a family-physician search to take several months in British Columbia.

Steve wanted to retire from psychiatric care—to show a degree of wellness. He may also have realized he needed more in-depth medical care. He and Dr. P had established that lithium carbonate, used in treating manic symptoms of hyperactivity, rushed speech, poor judgment, aggression and anger, and a reduced need for sleep, would best "tone down his engine" (as Dr. P had said). He could get that from a family doctor.

While we waited for blood tests and stool tests, eyesight issues suddenly seemed straightforward.

%%

According to Betty Edwards, there are five perceptual skills required in drawing: "the perception of edges...spaces...relationships...lights and shadows [and] of the whole."[84]

That wholeness of each of Steve's pieces of art expressed more than a summation of parts. Drawing *perceptually* consumed Steve's right brain while appeasing disturbance on the left. A healing wave welled up from Art's therapeutic power. Trouble was, the wave was a rogue.

Edwards described drawing as a magical process: "When your brain is weary of its verbal chatter, drawing is a way to quiet the chatter and to grasp a fleeting glimpse of transcendent reality....Visual perceptions stream through...retinas, optic pathways, brain hemispheres, motor pathways...to a direct image of your unique response.... Furthermore, drawing can reveal much about you to yourself, some facets of you that might be obscured by your verbal self."[85]

Steve had come to appreciate his artistic self. That he was more than his troubled thoughts, more than his erratic words, was reassuring: his true self, quietly coming into focus.

Elyn Saks, a professor of law, psychology, psychiatry and the behavioural sciences—and a lifelong schizophrenia sufferer (she dislikes the term schizophrenic)—comments on keeping occupied: "Being...productive...gives me great personal satisfaction. Also, it is one of the strongest weapons in my arsenal for keeping my psychosis at bay—when I am thinking, much of the crazy stuff recedes to the sidelines."[86]

This became clear to me and to those who viewed Steve's art, and eventually it became clear to Steve himself. He had found his essence in the stillness of meaningful work.

He had also found peace in the right-here-and-now brain, where insightful leaps abounded.

Spiritual teacher and author Eckhart Tolle says, "God or your essential nature...can be known, simply, easily, in the silent space of stillness....No matter how heavy and turbulent the mental, emotional noise may be...the stillness of pure consciousness...[is] not separate from the essence of the universe."[87]

Steve had first found elemental space in his work, then in himself. Some months earlier, he'd sat down to draw. Agitated, he'd said aloud in a stage whisper, "Shut the f—k up." I realized he wasn't speaking to me or to anyone in the studio. He was blocking out a hallucination so that he could begin sketching, unimpeded. Seconds later he was blocking in the figure of the model.

And this thing that people with schizophrenia lack? Insight—that is, being able to grasp the inner nature of people and situations?

One time, he asked to borrow my drawings. I was flattered at first until I realized he wanted his psychiatrist to psychoanalyze my sketches. Was he testing me or the doctor? Or his own perceptions of us both? Steve and I had, after all, sketched for the same time period and with the same materials—our differing perceptions of the same model, side by side.

"No, Steve. You may not take my art and pretend it's yours for Dr. P's analysis!"

He looked sheepish. He didn't say, "Don't be a ninny."

It might have been interesting to be part of that experiment. It might have been...insightful.

⸻

Philosopher and poet Friedrich Nietzsche said, "The Great Man... is colder, harder, less hesitating, and without fear of opinion; he lacks...respectability and...everything that is the virtue of the herd. If he cannot lead, he goes alone...incommunicable; he finds it tasteless to be familiar....When not speaking to himself, he wears a mask. There is a solitude within him that is inaccessible to praise or blame."[88]

There it was again. Praise and blame. Steve worked at being that aloof man. His favourite mask was that of Clown, fool or trickster. And the most famous trickster of Steve's generation was Marcel Marceau, popularly known as Bip the Clown.

The author Neil Strauss once wrote, "The soul of a mime is a complex one, part child and part artist, part clown and part tragic figure."[89]

Bip's "art of silence" or "styled pantomimes," Marceau claimed, "speak to the soul...making comedy, tragedy, and romance, involving you and your life...creating character and space...a whole show... showing our lives, our dreams, our expectations."[90]

When Steve was drawing, he became that silent, still and peacefully playful man.

⸻

Clown Villanelle
The look of the clown suited you
With glasses, moustaches, beards or dyed hair—
That slapstick witty point of view.

What's a myopic schizophrenic supposed to do
With fear and confusion—hallucinogenic fare?
The look of the clown suited you.

※

Most times when Steve and I arrived at Oakridge Centre, I went to the washroom and he waited for me near the children's play area. Invariably, he carried a toy in his pocket. He loved dollar-store or Value Village toys and marvelled at how they were made...at how everything was made. He interacted with toys as if laying out an elaborate picnic. The children would buzz around the play pit like bees around a hive, and they would hover around Steve's toy. In looking at them, I felt sure Steve saw the the toddler faces of his own children, lost to him long ago.

Steve the Clown surprised me on his arrival at Basic Inquiry wearing the mime's whiteface powder and shoe-polished hair. The room was warm to accommodate the model. Steve was sweating in his multi-layered clothing, and the shoe polish ran in streaks down his face, like runny makeup.

Two of his portraits wear a clown's nose, and he twice wore a clown mask, complete with red wig, to the art session. Steve's wooden clown head rests on my desk, and I rub his red nose for good luck. Maybe he and Steve shared some sweet silences and the odd guffaw.

"Steve, you have a smooth complexion and thick hair...no need for makeup," I'd say by way of discouraging this bizarre costume. That red-nosed, white-powder-faced clown helped Steve through his days, his weeks and perhaps his last months of life. He needed a few tricks up his sleeve.

※

With gymnastic skill and artistry too,
You applied your powder with debonair—
That slapstick witty point of view.

Your foes imagined, your friends were few—
Bip's Art of Silence you did wear—
The look of the clown suited you.

%

He'd had only two visits with the new GP. On the second visit, the doctor probed the mass. Steve weighed in at a stocky 205 pounds, but he'd already lost about twenty pounds. A mid-August blood-and-breath test showed slight anemia, but his blood pressure was good. Ten weeks later, he'd drop another fifty pounds.

When I expressed concern to Darren, he said, "What do you mean he's losing weight? He's got a gut."

His abdomen was bloated. It was easy to assume Steve was bigger than he was—like a bird's puffed-up feathers warding off the cold. A big tough guy, warding off the world.

"No, he's not fat. He's losing weight," I said. "Look at his face, his shoulders."

Sim, a retired nurse at Basic Inquiry, had pointed this out to me, but by then the weight was falling off him. Steve and I continued to sketch Tuesdays at Basic, although I picked him up at his place to conserve his energy. Into September, he stopped eating solids; I got high-calorie drinks at Safeway while Steve waited in the car.

"Those drinks are a lifesaver," he said.

I didn't think so. He got thinner.

"Why are you losing so much weight, my friend?" asked Bernie, one of the artists at Basic.

"I've been wrestling with a water buffalo," Steve answered. Bernie seemed to understand.

The water buffalo was his cancerous foe—the orc of orcs.

※

Much as Canada's medical system is touted for its efficiency, there's an uncertain time zone between a GP's suspicions and a referral to a specialist. The wait time can take several months, as was the case with Steve's late-summer referral to a gastrointestinal specialist. He was also wait-listed for an ultrasound and a computerized tomography (CT) scan.

In the meantime, the summer steamed ahead. September got even hotter. Steve's upstairs apartment trapped the heat. Ken and I passed by Steve's place on our way home from kayaking in the Fraser River estuary. I dropped off a tall drink through the veranda door's broken pane of glass. More and more, I found an excuse to drop by. This particular day, I wondered where Steve was. Later, I got the answer.

"I went to buy grapes," he told me from Vancouver General Hospital. I couldn't believe he'd venture a half-hour from home, on and off a bus, in his weakened condition. When he got home, he had fainted, according to landlord Lawrence, who called 911 and us.

Over a two-week stay, the medical team drained Steve's swollen belly, cleared pneumonia from his lungs with antibiotics and analyzed lymph. They did a biopsy, an ultrasound, a guided CT scan—none of their probes, scans or fluid analyses changed what the senior emergency doctor said that first night in admission: "This is a grave condition."

He was able to eat things like cream of wheat and chocolate pudding and sip on some tea.

Rod and his wife flew to Vancouver. They'd been hoping for a brotherly visit like one we'd had six years previous, visiting Stanley Park and playing bocce. They hadn't planned on a hospital visit.

This wasn't a cancer car chase; this was a cancer car crash. Steve had been totalled. The cancer source was in the large bowel or colon, metastasized in his lung (thus the pneumonia) and in the abdomen. I hadn't felt the car swerve, the brakes fail or the wheels give way. I hadn't realized that the pinworms he talked about were the attacking cancer cells.

"Good thing the doctor already spoke to me," said Steve as he, Darren and I returned from a medical-team meeting at the end of his hospital stay. It was the end of September. They suggested he had several months to live; it turned out to be several weeks.

"You definitely knew something was wrong," I told Steve.

He'd heard me describe my husband's hospitalization for the removal of a tumour in his transverse colon. The intervention meant a year of weekly chemotherapy and a slow recovery process. But Steve didn't want intervention. He wanted to be in the driver's seat (even if it was a broken-down jalopy), and he wanted to go home rather than to a hospice. Just before the opening of his second exhibit, he did just that.

"Joan, open a dictionary for the first two words you find," Steve had said earlier that summer about naming the show. "I have enough to do." I flipped open the dictionary—twice. I plugged my finger onto the page. The first word was *reformative*. The second was *destruct*. I wrote down the words and looked at them.

"*Re-formative De-struct*...what kind of an art show title is that?"

It came to me that a *destruct* wasn't necessarily a self-destruct but rather an unmaking: an undoing, an ending. And *reformative*, or its root verb *reform*, is to change or improve for the better, often associated with vice. Steve had worked with vices, or vises—filing, hammering and sawing woodwork and metal pieces. Steve's illness had him in a vice. There was no moral fault or blame.

Art Folio was my addition to the show's title, *Art Folio: Re-formative De-struct*. Mum had put aside Steve's art portfolio, as mothers do with keepsakes. Two feet high by one foot wide, the cover read: Art Folio. Steve's name was neatly inscribed in black within a circle of eyes and animals. Inside the folio were some of his early sketch assignments: hand and figure paintings, several paint abstracts mounted on construction paper. Disturbing titles like *Solitary Confinement, Midnight Sounds* and, the one that bothered me most, *Cry in the Wilderness*, a five-by-eight-inch canvas in dark paint with a tiny central pencil figure, arms open wide in supplication.

His first print was dated December 15, 1969. He'd done it at the Vancouver School of Art. He was twenty-one. He had left home three years earlier.

※

We prepared Steve's home as best we could. Darren refurbished it while Steve was in hospital: a new fridge stocked with easy-to-digest food, a new stove and microwave, new towels and bed linens. Molly Maid cleaners scrubbed the place spotless. And yet, his living space wasn't the main thing reformed.

Steve came to the Saturday show opening with Darren; he rested on a stool, sipping water. He accepted praise. He was gracious. By Tuesday, he wasn't strong enough to do more than a ten-minute sketch. I took him home.

※

Tragicomic characters emerged anew
With each sure stroke, you did bare
That slapstick witty point of view.

Melancholic triumph did imbue
The figures extraordinaire.
The look of the clown suited you—
That slapstick witty point of view.

%

Friday, I picked up the glasses and took Steve to an eye specialist friend. She was unaware of his terminal diagnosis and had given the appointment as a favour. I was reaching for something to get better for Steve. She checked his eyesight.

"Too clouded with glaucoma," she said. "Not a good candidate for surgery."

"Never mind," I said.

The idea of prescription glasses and getting an eye test had been important for such a long time. Now that idea was pointless. We got back in the car. We were near Stanley Park. I pulled up alongside the Sylvia Hotel with its ivied brick wall covered in lustrous red rubies.

"Look up, Steve," I said.

He looked. He said nothing. Was it bittersweet? For vision impairment to move toward improvement takes time and energy. Steve had neither.

We drove west along Vancouver's waterfront beaches, as if going backwards in time, along Forty-First Avenue to Trafalgar. I turned left. Past the church of our youth and up the three blocks to what had been our home property. A Pacific dogwood, British Columbia's floral emblem, had stood on the corner of the lot. It was gone, fallen to a fungus: a leaf blotch.

Those were the sidewalks and streets of our youth, where we'd climbed trees and ridden our bikes beyond the range of our mother's soprano supper call.

Circles began from there: the seven stones dropped in a pond. Each stone—an upward spurt of life force. Our circles rippled outward, collided, created new patterns and returned to stillness.

Did the glasses make seeing better? He kept them near. He cherished them. He'd wanted to see if prescription glasses made a difference. What made a difference may have been the caring.

%

A doctor friend advised me some weeks earlier to be vigilant for Steve's signs of demise.

In a journal on end-of-life care by doctoral nurses, one study participant said, "Death is the most critical point of illness. We must learn to treat [death] with [the] dignity and respect it deserves."[91]

Critical care professionals suggest making the environment as comfortable as possible. We'd done that. No patient should face death alone, yet in respect for the patient's wishes, they suggest managing pain and discomfort. This part was discomforting for me, as Steve wanted no pain management whatsoever. He'd refused palliative care treatment. He was speeding toward Mary Oliver's "cottage of darkness."

The following Wednesday, I went by Steve's on my way to a UBC creative non-fiction course that I'd signed up for some months earlier...writing true stories. I checked in on Steve on my way. The evening's theme was memoir and memory mapping—what we owed to the truth and what it meant to remember. It was only the second session; we were to write a filmable scene. Nothing came to me like the scene Steve had painted a half-hour earlier.

%

On the way to his place, halfway to UBC, I bought miso soup for Steve and sushi for myself.

I announced myself through his front door's broken pane of glass. The lock was so stiff; it was nearly impossible to enter. Darren and I had copied keys. I shouted from the foot of the stairs. "Steve?"

"Come on up," I heard him reply. He was lying on his bed. It was dim. The light source was a partially painted-over window behind him. He directed me to sit in the doorway. I pulled a chair to where he pointed. I couldn't see him except in silhouette.

"Miso soup," he said. "That's salty, isn't it?" He took a sip. I sat there and chopsticked sushi into my mouth. I chewed. I swallowed. I said something. He regurgitated the soup within a minute of swallowing. Not noisily. He'd had a spit bottle handy these past two months.

"I'll be back on Friday afternoon, Steve." He reached for my hand. He'd never done that before.

Friday morning, Darren dropped by Steve's place. "Steve is okay," Darren said when we spoke on the phone. "You don't need to go; he's resting."

"I said I'd go, so I will."

By late Friday afternoon, the front door was ajar. It was warping. I pushed it open and went upstairs. There was no response to my shout from the foot of the stairs. He was in bed, restless and incoherent. He didn't know me. I called 911.

How to describe the condition of a loved one to a 911 operator? How to explain that this man has suffered too much? How to speak logistically when the heart is cracking?

The medic attended Steve in the small bedroom. One or two firefighters hovered in the cramped middle space of the kitchen, looking dubiously at paint tins. As they tilted him onto the stretcher and angled him downstairs, I told Steve, "I'll stay with you now." As we exited the front door, that threshold where we so often parted company, he lost consciousness. Even when he regained it a minute later, I knew he was slipping away.

"We're going to the hospital, where they can help you," I told him. I wasn't sure if Steve heard me or what help we would find there.

"Are you coming with us?" said the paramedic.

To Steve, I repeated, "I'll be right here."

The paramedics tried to inject him with something, but he held his arm in a tight arm lock.

"Call family members to meet you there," said the medic.

I held that hand that he'd offered me several days earlier. I was holding on. So was he.

Once we arrived at the hospital, Darren and Sally arrived. The doctor in charge had the same name as one of Steve's sons.

"Steve, this is Dr. M. He's going to give you something to help." He was conscious but not speaking. They gave him an opioid and he fell into a deep sleep. I rested my hand on the back of his neck.

His skinny arm was riveted in an L-shape, bent ninety degrees at the elbow. He'd turned onto his side, facing me, although my chair was positioned nearer his chest since there was a bedside table opposite his face. The doctor suggested an IV. He wasn't sure the injection would flow past Steve's locked arm.

Darren, Sally and I told Steve he was our beloved artist brother, free to pastel sunrises and sunsets with the sky as his canvas, no longer tied to his pain: free to soar—permission given, leave to let go. Steve's breath came more quietly. Within the hour, with the three of us around him, his breathing stopped.

A social worker came in some minutes later and asked if we'd consider donating Steve's corneas.

"Steve had beautiful eyes," said Darren. He touched Steve's hair.

"He had a lot of challenges with his eyes," I told the social worker.

"That won't be a factor," she said.

"Then that would be beautiful." We all agreed.

※

I'd been stumped by the voracity and suddenness of the cancer. What's left when an old-growth tree is cut down? A stump. This tree of a man was gone.

"I'm sorry you're so sick," I had said while he and I sat on the bottom steps in the waning October light.

"You've been an angel," he murmured. That was the first compliment he'd ever bestowed upon me. Like a benediction.

I have always believed humans can be angels for one other. Seeming strangers can step in and step up. I suppose that was part of my initial involvement with Steve—thinking I could help him. It soon became clear that he had so much to offer me and so much to show me that I hadn't seen before.

Some quirk of dispositions meant we could be there for each other, despite the years we had spent apart. There was enough common ground, once we'd filled in the gaps.

////

A blending stump was one of Steve's least favourite tools. Made from tightly wound soft paper, it is a cylindrical smudge tool for graphite, charcoal, chalk pastel or Conté crayon. The gradations and halftones it delineates were not details Steve saw. A damp tea bag would do. He went for the big picture.

CHAPTER 10

Kneaded Erasures

HISTORIAN SIR ANTHONY KENNY translated the most influential book on poetry ever written. And yet, there are no poems in *Poetics* by Aristotle. However, Kenny brought Aristotle's philosophy to modern consciousness from 300 BCE.

Kenny split the slippery beast of *poiesis* into two tamer beasts in describing it as a hybrid between prose fiction and verse, best exemplified by tragedy, the Greeks' most famous literary form. Represented here is prose fiction, verse and tragic tale; the latter, according to Aristotle, should end happily.

"The Greeks came to the plays in order to weep together...[to] strengthen the bond....Art helps...to realize that we are not alone: everybody else is suffering too."[92]

Together we are able to purge pity and fear, and come away emotionally stronger.

Kenny chose the word "representation" to best exemplify imitation, miming or *mimesis*.

But "representation cannot stand alone,"[93] says California painter Sandra Mendelsohn, who goes on to say, "True poetry lies in the orchestration of a good composition combined with the skillful use of paint and color, all driven by sensory perception, intuition and memory." That is in effect what we have here. Steve's paint and colour, and my memories.

There are two parts to the bridge that Steve and I built: *mimesis* in the doing of the art form (Steve's artistic pilings and footings— the substructure of the bridge), and *poiesis* in the making of the story, with its style and ideas (my girders and guardrails— the superstructure of the bridge). Steve and I spanned a giant see-saw of counterweights and balances—his in the doing, mine in the making. All was a result of his doing-action. Steve allowed his personal bridge to be drawn aside in pursuit of the artful bond between us.

"Steve, you *do* the art," I had said. "I'll do the rest."

Representational art is exemplified in figures, landscapes and still life. Representational artists paint, draw and sculpt real-life subjects (repeatedly, as the prefix suggests). For Steve, drawing the human figure was his key act of representation—his act of doing.

Aristotle wrote that humans make things in order to interpret their world. This remaking of Steve's artful doing is my way of interpreting his transformation.

Aristotle may have been the first to write of representational practice, even though cavemen had painted cave walls many millennia before the Greek Golden Age. Impressionists and Expressionists painted canvases, marvelling at what the Greeks had done (yet like all artists, they wanted to surpass them).

Steve set it down in the mixed media of chalk pastel, charcoal and Conté crayon. In so doing, he found his true nature. He bloomed and unfurled it.

I'm reminded of Shams, a thirteenth-century Persian poet and seeker, who taught Rumi to see and represent the world around him:

The writing comes in three scripts:
One that he and only he can read.
One that he and others can read.
One that neither he nor anyone else can read.
I am that third script.[94]

When Rumi first met Shams, Shams allegedly asked Rumi what he was reading. Rumi, a scholar, suggested it was beyond Shams's understanding, since he was a humble basket weaver, upon which Shams grabbed Rumi's book and threw it into a fountain. Rumi fished it out and asked Shams why he had done that. Shams suggested that all of Rumi's learning could not begin to fathom what is incomprehensible. Rumi spent a good part of his life (seventy thousand verses' worth) deciphering his mentor's meaning.

Steve opened to me an artful yet non-verbal sphere. It was here that he freely expressed himself.

I started out as Steve's rep, but he became mine. To represent an image or likeness, either in word or sketch, requires that the rep or spokesperson, in the act of representing, avows truth as sworn testimony. Creative non-fiction—whether poetry, travelogue or personal-essay writing—is a similar act of representation.

"Why should I seek? I am the same as He. His essence speaks through me. I have been looking for myself!"[95]

Shams said as much in three scripts or truths. Steve's first truth along our voyage was finding a personal identity. In restoring what was lost so many times in wallets and carry bags, Steve got an ID card for the voting process. It was part of becoming a card-carrying member of society.

American essayist Henry David Thoreau said, "All voting is a sort of gaming, like checkers or backgammon, with a slight moral tinge to it, a playing with right and wrong."[96] Steve wanted to play.

Rumi wrote, in Persian, five couplets called ghazals. My ghazal to Steve is represented here:

Thirteenth-century Sufi poet Rumi penned ghazals
In five couplets or shers: each, a stand-alone.

An equal rhythm: loving one-liner
Ending in tender dedication.

Rumi mourned and searched for Shams, his spiritual teacher
Now you are gone, Artful Stepping Stone: seer, friend.

Your quest is now mine to search for and quantify
In that third mystery: to find, to have and hone.

Representation: the essence of the
Creative artist, Stephen Alexander Corcoran.

%

Steve needed ID to vote. Since 1988, the Council of Canadians with Disabilities has used the Canadian Charter of Rights and Freedoms to challenge voter exclusion and enable over fifty thousand Canadians living with mental illness to vote. For the federal election of May 2011, I vouched for Steve, and he brought two official envelopes from the government that had been addressed to him. For this and the Vancouver municipal election of November 2011, we voted at the school gym near his home. He participated in a choosing ritual.

By May of 2013, the British Columbia provincial election was about to happen. Steve was one of the first Vancouverites to apply for and use the new identity card, combining a (non-driver's) licence and health services card with photo identification. With this BC Services Card, Steve was proud to vote. Neither of our chosen candidates got into office, yet we still shared in the electoral process. He had a voice.

※

My friend had asked Steve at that chance meeting what sort of art he did. He didn't know what to make of that question. What to do with it?

Like Shams said, it's up to others to determine or interpret meaning, to make of it what they will. Steve took advantage of an opportunity to benefit from his artful talent. Art speaks for itself, just as Ann had said that Steve's pieces were in a dialogue all their own.

Given the right occasion, it's what you do with it that counts. Steve was that artful doer.

Steve's art has become part of the Art Rental Programme at North Vancouver Community Arts Council (now North Van Arts). By contracting it out to movie sets, as well as to community members to rent or purchase, North Van Arts upholds the promise that is his work. He and I took the SeaBus to North Vancouver one day in his final months, walking the four blocks slowly uphill, to see his work on display. He was unimpressed. The beauty for him was in the doing.

※

The gap in the two-way mirror between Steve and me dissolves. We each turn out to be part hero, part mentor, part helper and part hinderer, like everyone else.

Steve's triumph came in artful realization. The Vancouver School of Art that he attended in the late 1960s became the Emily Carr University of Art and Design (ECUAD). The Stephen A. Corcoran Memorial Award[97] is an ECUAD bursary given every spring to a student coping with a significant and chronic mental health challenge. Steve's bursary is the first of its kind at ECUAD.

There are more than two hundred kinds of mental illness, so bursary recipients might be dealing with any combination of manic or depressed states of bipolar disorder, anxiety disorder, personality disorder, and obsessive-compulsive disorder (OCD); learning or mood disorders; or post-traumatic stress disorder. All beneficiaries of the bursary proactively manage their lives with regular schedules, set tasks and positive regimens of healthy diets and regular exercise. Some are advocates for their peers while continuing to seek personal counselling from their doctors and health professionals while combatting lifelong challenges.

Mental health challenges affect one in five (over seven million) Canadians, according to the Canadian Mental Health Association. The National Institute of Mental Health contends that over forty million people in the US live with mental illness. The remaining 80 percent might be compelled to *do* something about it—or to *make* something of it.

※

Along with twenty-five other kayakers, Ken and I launch from Harrison Hot Springs toward the western side of Harrison Lake, where we find entry to Harrison River, a kilometre away.

It is one week after my brother's death when we kayak down this waterway, the largest salmon-producing tributary of the Fraser River. Paddling the river is an analogous balm. Nature unburdens a heavy heart whenever I follow my own rhythmic breathing. In our double kayak, Ken and I are part of a convoy: flowing downstream at two and a half knots. There is one knot in my chest that won't go away.

Steve's journey upstream started when metastasized colon cancer cut off his nutrient flow. He entered the freshwater stage when salmon fin upstream without eating. Flesh loses oil, substance. Yet salmon are a keystone species, and relative to their biomass, they have a strong impact through the nutrients they leave behind.

"Don't remember me this way," Steve had said of his wasted condition. What I remember is his purpose and strength in adversity. Nothing wasted there.

We are running the river to see salmon swim upstream that final leg. It is fall, a time for harvesting and gathering. Orange, yellow and purple leaves reflect in the hues of life jackets, paddles and boats. The female salmon makes up to seven redds or nests into which she deposits five thousand pea-sized eggs. Steve and I were of the same nest.

Our nest was a Celtic one, and in Irish mythology, salmon are sacred: venerable and wise. In the legend *Boyhood Deeds of Fionn*,[98] young Fionn is cooking the Salmon of Wisdom for his teacher-sage, Finn Eces, who hopes to glean all the wisdom of the world from eating it. In the cooking process, young Fionn burns his thumb on the fish. He puts his thumb in his mouth to soothe the pain, and thereby gains the entire world's knowledge. My brother drew artistic wisdom from the ancestral thumb.

Given a chance, Steve wanted to work out issues. Argue. He'd often say, "The argument is, Joan..."

I'd say, "I don't want an argument." I now believe he meant to talk over ways and means—looking upstream.

※

Steve's art washes into a creative estuary. His art nourishes with hope. From fry stage, the up-and-comers wind their way to where the real migration begins.

The river's burble is our dialogue. We paddle in shallow water, keeling over our hips. If we were on gravel, we'd be spawning. Against the flow, the salmon surface. They splash. They struggle. They die. They remind us of our own lives, full of challenge and opportunity.

We land for lunch on the sandy confluence of Morris Creek on the west bank of the Harrison. Behind us are pictographs on the granite's pale surface: shamanic figures, visual poetry from the Sts'ailes Nation (formerly Chehalis) ancestral scribes. Artists find an outlet, an inlet, a river of representative energy.

The fish-carcass stench is pungent. Strewn along the shore are five kinds of salmon. We are in an odd year, 2013: a good one for pinks. Chum, coho and chinook join the chorus. Sockeye add rouge to the river's pockmarked cheeks in this, a predominant year.

Steve was the king or chinook: I, his chum. Kings are known for their size but also for being the earliest to return to their spawning channels. Forerunners. Perhaps that's why they are endangered.

※

A month later, family members gathered at Basic Inquiry for Steve's memorial. Ken and I, Steve's three sons, my sister Sally, my brother Darren, and their partners, friends and children. Father Bob welcomed us. I read aloud: "January would have been ten years of Tuesdays for me with Steve, and this November 10, his sixty-fifth birthday. He wasn't destined to be a senior citizen—he was a hippie at heart." I was shaky. My voice catching. Father Bob put a hand on my shoulder. I pressed on, even though I felt sure I'd failed to sum Steve up: "He'd grown layers of resilience that reflected in the multi-layered clothing he wore…the hats, the jackets. The black leather one, his elephant skin…He never doubted that he was an artist; he doubted whether he could fit in."

That group in which he feared he couldn't function weighed in.

The members at Basic Inquiry attested to Steve's gift—how he enlivened the studio with his expressionistic impressions. They spoke of his talent, his inventive energy.

James, the current session manager, lightened the sombre mood saying how Steve always got the better of me. (I hope he got my best.)

Another James recounted how he met Steve one Tuesday when I wasn't at the session. He was a new member, newly arrived: "I was a bit alarmed to see him…I didn't know Steve's name…I thought he was a street guy. I was going to alert the session manager when I noticed how expertly he set up his easel. Then, the quick sketches began. I stood back. Steve was intent on the model. At the break, I stole over to have a peek…I was blown away. His work was the real deal. He was the real deal."

※

Steve didn't want erasure and, like many artists, he didn't erase. A soft eraser moulds, textures and highlights pieces of art. Used in subtractive drawing, a kneaded or putty eraser pulls to capacity, blotting or lightening the line. It shades without wiping out. Over time, erasers lose their efficacy. Without smearing or damaging the paper, they pick up particles and deform. Steve had reached that capacity.

We buried Steve's urn on the edge of a forest above a sports field at North Vancouver Cemetery. Darren and his wife, and Sally and I read a tribute to Steve (and his hobbit hanger-on, Bilbo). Bilbo had given Steve the ring. In turn, he'd passed it along to his chum.

※

The Road goes ever on and on
Out from the door where it began.
Now far ahead the Road has gone.
Let others follow, if they can!

Let them a journey new begin.
But I at last with weary feet
Will turn toward the lighted inn,
My evening rest and sleep to meet.[99]

////

For us, drawing was a bridge thread that spanned mental illness. Sometimes a bridge is enough between one person and another. But the bridge is not the web.

"How It Works in 30 Seconds"[100] shows how spiders cast a bridge thread until they find an anchor. They then go back and forth to reinforce it. That was Steve and I the first two years of our reunion. Back and forth. Back and forth. Looking for a way across the bridge, but there was a gap. The spider lets her weight drop the thread down (in Steve's case, the body of his artwork) to radiate outward and spiral the web from the inside out. From the inside out was how our web formed—drawing together within artistic communities, where we became enmeshed.

Darwin's bark spider[101] spans rivers up to twenty-five metres across. If an interloper messes up her bridge strand, she bites it off, reels it in and eats it. She casts multiple lines, like a hip-wading flyfisher. She's as wily a web thrower as Charlotte, who said, "No, my webs were no miracle, Wilbur. I was only describing what I saw. The miracle is you...I also made you a promise to save your life. But how? With the right words you can change the world."[102] Charlotte might have mentioned something about how words aren't the only way: that making art can also significantly shake things up. Or playing bocce. Or any of the myriad of non-verbal activities that hinge and pivot, raise and lower barriers to communication. No moat too wide. No castle or tower too impenetrable. I can now connect those dots.

Steve's bridge was Kevlar-strong, just like the bark spider's. He cast it. I caught it. So did others. His work wound its way into the web of the Art Studios, Basic Inquiry, the North Vancouver Community Arts Council (North Van Arts) and the Emily Carr University of Art and Design. Sticky filaments catch on.

The nineteenth-century Romantic painter Eugène Delacroix said, "I have told myself a hundred times that painting—that is, the material thing called a painting—is no more than a pretext, the bridge between the mind of the painter and that of the spectator."[103]

Steve's art gave him the opportunity to draw figures, to observe and draw those doing the drawing, to observe his and their work, and sometimes, to include in the drawing, the art on a gallery wall. Casting, spinning, bridging, spanning, creating a web—

Art raised us up and provided passage.

NOTES

1 Robert Henri, "On Drawing," in *The Art Spirit* (New York: Basic Books, 2007), 242. (First published by J.B. Lippincott Company, 1923.)

2 J.R.R. Tolkien, *The Hobbit* (London: HarperCollins Publishers, 2003).

3 "Steve Jobs' Speech at Stanford University," Obituaries, National Public Radio, October 6, 2011, https://www.npr.org/2011/10/06/141122856/steve-jobs-speech-at-stanford-university.

4 Peter Morrell, "'Family Dynamics and the Third Child as Outsider," July 1999, http://www.homeoint.org/morrell/misc/thirdchild.htm.

5 Pema Chodron, *When Things Fall Apart: Heart Advice for Difficult Times* (Boulder: Shambhala Publications, 2016), 63.

6 Chodron, 63.

7 John Nash, "Famous People Who Hear Voices," Hearing Voices Network, https://www.hearing-voices.org/about-voices/famous-people/.

8 Christel Broederlow, "What Is an Empath?," ThoughtCo., updated August 17, 2017, https://www.thoughtco.com/traits-of-empaths-1724671.

9 Aron, Elaine. *The Highly Sensitive Person: How to Thrive When the World Overwhelms You* (New York: Broadway Books, 1996).

10 Ryszard Kapuściński, *The Other* (London: Verso, 2008).

11 "An Interview with Ryszard Kapuściński: Writing about Suffering," *The Journal of the International Institute* 6, no. 1 (Fall 1998), https://quod.lib.umich.edu/j/jii/4750978.0006.107/--interview-with-ryszard-kapuscinski-writing-about-suffering?rgn=main;view=fulltext.

12 Roman Krznaric, *Empathy: Why It Matters, and How to Get It* (New York: TarcherPerigee, 2015).

13 "Freddy the Freeloader: Red Skeleton's Famous Hobo Clown," Famous Clowns, September 4, 2011, https://famousclowns.org/red-skelton/freddy-the-freeloader-red-skeltons-famous-hobo-clown/.

14 "Ten Things Chris Hadfield Can't Live Without," *Toronto Life*, November 6, 2014, https://torontolife.com/city/chris-hadfield-the-list/.

15 Mark Evanier, *Mad Art: A Visual Celebration of the Art of* Mad Magazine *and the Idiots Who Create It* (New York: Watson-Guptill, 2002).

16 Joe Castaldo, "The Teenage Brain on Weed," *Maclean's*, February 2018, 35.

17 Plato, *The Republic*, bk. 7.

18 "Anosognosia," National Alliance on Mental Illness, https://www.nami.org/ Learn-More/Mental-Health-Conditions/Related-Conditions/Anosognosia.

19 A song that's been performed in countless Muppet productions, although I know it from the Snoopy musical. Hal Clayton Hackady and Larry Grossman, "If Just One Person Believes in You" (Los Angeles: Warner/Chappell Music, 1975).

20 For more information on how medication can help those suffering with schizophrenia manage their illness, see: "Voices: Living with Schizophrenia | WebMD," WebMD, October 12, 2017, https://www.youtube.com/watch?v=C7Jl9_59tfY&feature=youtu.be.

21 Ingrid Waldron, "Communicating with a Loved One Who Has a Mental Illness," Main Line PA, National Alliance on Mental Illness, https://namipamainline.org/ communicating-with-a-loved-one-who-has-a-mental-illness/.

22 "The Art Studios," Recovery Through Art, http://recoverythroughart.ca/ the-art-studios/.

23 Raphael Underwood, "Lithium for Schizophrenia: Cochrane Find Lack of Evidence to Support Its Use," National Elf Service, https://www.nationalelfservice.net/mental-health/schizophrenia/ lithium-for-schizophrenia-cochrane-find-lack-of-evidence-to-support-its-use/.

24 Underwood.

25 Kevin Eastman and Peter Laird, *Teenage Mutant Ninja Turtles* (New York: Mirage Studios).

26 Betty Edwards, *The New Drawing on the Right Side of the Brain*, revised edition (New York: TarcherPedigree, 1999), 221.

27 Edwards.

28 Nick Bantock, *The Artful Dodger: Images and Reflections* (San Francisco: Chronicle Books, 2000), 90.

29 Mihaly Csikszentmihalyi, *Flow: The Psychology of Optimal Experience* (Harper Perennial Modern Classics, 2008).

30 Betty Edwards, *Drawing on the Right Side of the Brain*, revised edition (New York: Penguin Putnam, 1989).

31 Edwards, *Drawing on the Right Side of the Brain*, xiii.

32 Edwards, *Drawing on the Right Side of the Brain*, 42.

33 Basic Inquiry: The Vancouver Life Drawing Society, http://www.lifedrawing.org/index.html.

34 Susan A. Sternau, *Henri Matisse* (New York: Todtri, 1997), 70.

35 Claude Allemand-Cosneau, Manfred Fath and David Mitchinson, *Henry Moore: From the Inside Out* (Munich: Prestel, 2009), 12.

36 Allemand-Cosneau et al., 132.

37 Roger Benjamin, *Matisse's "Notes of a Painter": Criticism, Theory, and Context, 1891–1908* (Umi Research Press, 1987).

38 Klaus Reichold and Bernhard Graf, *Paintings That Changed the World: From Lascaux to Picasso* (Prestel, 2010).

39 Tate (website), https://www.tate.org.uk/art/art-terms/f/figurative-art.

40 "ABC Wide World Classic 'The Agony of Defeat' Vinko Bogataj Interview," presented by Brent Musburger, 1997, https://www.youtube.com/watch?v=n_ZvwIFbXMM.

41 Sylvia Nasar, *A Beautiful Mind* (New York: Simon & Schuster, 1998), 97.

42 William Kluba, *Where Does Art Come From? How to Find Inspiration and Ideas* (New York: Allworth, 2014), 99.

43 Edwards, *Drawing on the Right Side of the Brain*.

44 Isabelle Julia, ed., *The Modern Woman: Drawings by Degas, Renoir, Toulouse-Lautrec and Other Masterpieces from the Musée D'Orsay, Paris* (Vancouver Art Gallery, 2010), 17. Published in conjunction with an exhibition of the same title, organized by the Vancouver Art Gallery and Musée D'Orsay and presented at the Vancouver Art Gallery.

45 Hazel Harrison, *Pastel School* (New York: Reader's Digest Association, 1996), 4–5.

46 Harrison, 8.

47 Harrison, 26.

48 Harrison, 34.

49 Harrison, 64.

50 Harrison, 86.

51 Harrison, 88.

52 Kimon Nicolaides, *The Natural Way to Draw: A Working Plan for Art Study* (Boston: Mariner Books, 1990), 9.

53 Nicolaides, 10.

54 Nicolaides, 16.

55 Nicolaides, 221.

56 Kenneth Clark, *The Nude: A Study in Ideal Form* (Princeton: Princeton University Press, 1956), 8.

57 Clark, 3.

58 Clark, 370.

59 Clark, 29.

60 Clark, 358.

61 John Berger, Sven Blomberg, Chris Fox, Michael Dibb and Richard Hollis, *Ways of Seeing* (London: British Broadcasting Corporation and Penguin Books, 1972), 10.

62 Glenn McNatt, "Photography and Painting Influence Each Other," *Baltimore Sun*, February 15, 1998, https://www.baltimoresun.com/news/bs-xpm-1998-02-15-1998046086-story.html.

63 McNatt.

64 Clark.

65 Leo Tolstoy, *What Is Art?*, trans. Richard Pevear and Larissa Volokhonsky (London: Penguin, 1996).

66 BC Schizophrenia Society and F.O.R.C.E. Society for Kids Mental Health, *How You Can Help: A Toolkit for Families*, 2010, https://www.heretohelp.bc.ca/sites/default/files/images/family_toolkit_full.pdf.

67 BC Schizophrenia Society and F.O.R.C.E., 80.

68 Kenneth Grahame, *The Wind in the Willows* (North Yorkshire: Methuen Publishing, 1981).

69 Mark Twain, *The Adventures of Tom Sawyer* (New York: Penguin, 2006), 22.

70 Quoted in "Holding On and Hoarding," Brookhaven Hospital, October 24, 2013, http://www.brookhavenhospital.com/holding-on-and-hoarding/.

71 Charles Schultz, *Peanuts*, July 13, 1954. First comic strip series dialogue between characters Patty and Pigpen.

72 *Life*, April 19, 1963. Colgate toothpaste ad, page 55.

73 Berger et al., 46.

74 Sandra Yuen MacKay, *My Schizophrenic Life: The Road to Recovery from Mental Illness* (Dundas: Bridgeross Communications, 2010).

75 Bob Raczka, *Name That Style: All about Isms in Art* (Minneapolis: Millbrook Press, 2009).

76 Malcolm Gladwell, *Outliers: The Story of Success* (New York: Little, Brown and Company, 2010), 198.

77 Quoted in "Johanna van Gogh-Bonger," Wikipedia, https://en.wikipedia.org/wiki/Johanna_van_Gogh-Bonger#cite_note-3.

78 Wassily Kandinsky, *Concerning the Spiritual in Art* (New York: Dover Publications, 1977), vii.

79 "The Emotion Wheel: What Is It and How to Use It?," Positive Psychology Program, last updated February 14, 2019, https://positivepsychologyprogram.com/emotion-wheel/.

80 Roberta Jenkins, "Study Examines Why Left Cheek Portraits Appear Happier," PsyPost, April 3, 2017, https://www.psypost.org/2017/04/study-examines-left-cheek-portraits-appear-happier-48654.

81 Krznaric.

82 Nicolaides, 221.

83 Mary Oliver, "When Death Comes," *New and Selected Poems* (Boston: Beacon Press, 1992).

84 Edwards, xii.

85 Edwards, 222.

86 Elyn R. Saks, quoted in an interview with Dominic Fannon, "e-Interview," *The Psychiatrist* 35, no. 7 (July 2011): 280, https://doi.org/10.1192/pb.bp.111.035550.

87 Eckhart Tolle, "Your Essential Nature," April 28, 2011, http://spiritualtalks.com/eckhart-tolle-your-essential-nature.

88 Friedrich Nietzsche, *Thus Spoke Zarathustra: A Book for All and None*, trans. Walter Kaufmann, revised edition (New York: Modern Library, 1995), 11.

89 Neil Strauss, "The Pop Life: Michael Jackson's Sound of Silence," *New York Times*, December 21, 1995, https://www.nytimes.com/1995/12/21/arts/the-pop-life-michael-jackson-s-sound-of-silence.html.

90 "Marcel Marceau Remembered (CBS Sunday Morning)," September 25, 2007, video, 00:30, https://www.youtube.com/watch?v=QbxNWmH6CAo&feature=youtu.be.

91 Renea L. Beckstrand, Lynn Clark Callister and Karin T. Kirchhoff, "Providing a 'Good Death': Critical Care Nurses' Suggestions for Improving End-of-Life Care," American Journal of Critical Care 15, no. 1 (January 2006): 38–45, http://ajcc.aacnjournals.org/content/15/1/38.full?sid=3dfff1bd-3702-4add-bfad-9f192b4056de.

92 Karen Armstrong, *Twelve Steps to a Compassionate Life* (New York: Alfred A. Knopf, 2010), 93–98.

93 F. Scott Hess, "5 Artists on the Enduring Qualities of Representational Painting," *HuffPost*, updated December 6, 2017, https://www.huffingtonpost.com/f-scott-hess/5-artists-on-the-enduring_b_5826276.html.

94 Attributed to Shams-i-Tabrīzī, thirteenth-century Persian sage, on the aftermath of meeting the renowned poet Rumi.

95 Rumi, *The Essential Rumi*, trans. Coleman Barks (San Francisco: Harper, 1995), xx.

96 Henry David Thoreau, "Civil Disobedience," 1849, http://xroads.virginia.edu/~hyper2/thoreau/civil.html.

97 "2019 Stephen A. Corcoran Memorial Award," Emily Carr University, February 9, 2018, http://www.connect.ecuad.ca/about/news/340492.

98 "The Boyhood Deeds of Fionn," Wikipedia, https://en.wikipedia.org/wiki/The_Boyhood_Deeds_of_Fionn.

99 Tolkien. This song is sung many times throughout the journey in both *The Hobbit* and *The Lord of the Rings*.

100 "How Spiders Make Webs," howitworksmag, video, June 18, 2015, https://youtu.be/e6Sq7-_G-TA.

101 "Spider Shoots 25 Metre Web," BBC Earth, video, June 25, 2017, https://youtu.be/nlRkwuAcUd4.

102 E.B. White, *Charlotte's Web* (New York: HarperCollins, 2012).

103 Edwards, 219.

BIBLIOGRAPHY

"2019 Stephen A. Corcoran Memorial Award." Emily Carr University. February 9, 2018. http://www.connect.ecuad.ca/about/news/340492.

"ABC Wide World Classic 'The Agony of Defeat' Vinko Bogataj Interview." Presented by Brent Musburger. 1997. https://www.youtube.com/watch?v=n_ZvwIFbXMM.

Allemand-Cosneau, Claude, Manfred Fath and David Mitchinson. *Henry Moore: From the Inside Out.* Munich: Prestel, 2009.

Andre, Christophe. *Looking at Mindfulness: 25 Ways to Live in the Moment Through Art.* New York: Blue Rider Press, 2015.

"Anosognosia." National Alliance on Mental Illness. https://www.nami.org/Learn-More/Mental-Health-Conditions/Related-Conditions/Anosognosia.

Aristotle. *Poetics.* Trans. A. Kenny. Oxford: Oxford University Press, 2013.

Armstrong, Karen. *Twelve Steps to a Compassionate Life.* New York: Alfred A. Knopf, 2010.

Aron, Elaine. *The Highly Sensitive Person: How to Thrive When the World Overwhelms You.* New York: Broadway Books, 1996.

"The Art Studios." Recovery Through Art. http://recoverythroughart.ca/the-art-studios/.

Bantock, Nick. *The Artful Dodger: Images and Reflections.* San Francisco: Chronicle Books, 2000.

BC Schizophrenia Society and F.O.R.C.E. Society for Kids Mental Health. *How You Can Help: A Toolkit for Families.* 2010. https://www.heretohelp. bc.ca/sites/default/files/images/family_toolkit_full.pdf.

Beckstrand, Renea L., Lynn Clark Callister and Karin T. Kirchhoff. "Providing a 'Good Death': Critical Care Nurses' Suggestions for Improving End-of-Life Care." *American Journal of Critical Care* 15, no. 1 (January 2006). http://ajcc.aacnjournals.org/content/15/1/38. full?sid=3dfff1bd-3702-4add-bfad-9f192b4056de.

Benjamin, Roger. *Matisse's "Notes of a Painter": Criticism, Theory, and Context, 1891–1908.* Umi Research Press, 1987.

Berger, John, Sven Blomberg, Chris Fox, Michael Dibb and Richard Hollis. *Ways of Seeing.* London: British Broadcasting Corporation and Penguin Books, 1972.

Birren, Faber. *Color: A Survey in Words and Pictures, from Ancient Mysticism to Modern Science.* New York: University Books, 1963.

"The Boyhood Deeds of Fionn." Wikipedia. https://en.wikipedia.org/wiki/ The_Boyhood_Deeds_of_Fionn.

Braid, Kate, and Sandy Shreve. *In Fine Form: The Canadian Book of Form Poetry.* Halfmoon Bay: Caitlin Press, 2005.

Broederlow, Christel. "What Is an Empath?" ThoughtCo. August 17, 2017. https://www.thoughtco.com/traits-of-empaths-1724671.

Burnstein, Julie. *Spark: How Creativity Works.* New York: Harper, 2011.

Campbell, Joseph. *The Hero with a Thousand Faces.* Second ed. Princeton: Princeton University Press, 1968.

Castaldo, Joe. "The Teenage Brain on Weed." *Maclean's*, February 2018.

Chodron, Pema. *When Things Fall Apart: Heart Advice for Difficult Times.* Boulder: Shambhala Publications, 2016.

Clark, Kenneth. *The Nude: A Study in Ideal Form*. Princeton: Princeton University Press, 1956.

Cockburn, Patrick, and Henry Cockburn. *Henry's Demons: Living with Schizophrenia, a Father and Son's Story*. New York: Scribner, 2011.

Constance, Diana. *Complete Life Drawing Course*. New York: Sterling, 2001.

Csikszentmihalyi, Mihaly. *Flow: The Psychology of Optimal Experience*. Harper Perennial Modern Classics, 2008.

Eastman, Kevin, and Peter Laird. *Teenage Mutant Ninja Turtles*. New York: Mirage Studios, 1984–2010.

Edwards, Betty. *Drawing on the Right Side of the Brain*. Revised edition. New York: Penguin Putnam, 1989.

———. *The New Drawing on the Right Side of the Brain*. Revised edition. New York: TarcherPedigree, 1999.

"The Emotion Wheel: What Is It and How to Use It?" Positive Psychology Program. February 14, 2019. https://positivepsychologyprogram.com/emotion-wheel/.

Evanier, Mark. *Mad Art: A Visual Celebration of the Art of* Mad Magazine *and the Idiots Who Created It*. New York: Watson-Guptill, 2002.

Fannon, Dominic. "e-Interview." The Psychiatrist 35, no. 7 (July 2011): 280, https://doi.org/10.1192/pb.bp.111.035550.

Fields, R. Douglas. *The Other Brain: From Dementia to Schizophrenia, How New Discoveries about the Brain Are Revolutionizing Medicine and Science*. New York: Simon & Schuster, 2010.

Fisher, Jude. *The Fellowship of the Ring Visual Companion*. Boston: Houghton Mifflin Harcourt, 2001.

Foer, Jonathan Safran. *Everything Is Illuminated*. Boston: Houghton Mifflin, 2002.

"Freddy the Freeloader: Red Skelton's Famous Hobo Clown." Famous Clowns. September 4, 2011. https://famousclowns.org/red-skelton/freddy-the-freeloader-red-skeltons-famous-hobo-clown/.

Gaiman, Neil. *Make Good Art*. New York: William Morrow, 2013.

Gladwell, Malcolm. *Outliers: The Story of Success*. New York: Little, Brown and Company, 2010.

Gooch, Brad. *Rumi's Secret: The Life of the Sufi Poet of Love*. New York: HarperCollins, 2017.

Grahame, Kenneth. *The Wind in the Willows*. North Yorkshire: Methuen Publishing, 1981.

Grant, Adam. *Originals: How Non-Conformists Move the World*. New York: Viking, 2016.

Hackady, Hal Clayton, and Larry Grossman. "If Just One Person Believes in You." Los Angeles: Warner/Chappell Music, 1975.

Harrison, Hazel. *Pastel School*. New York: Reader's Digest Association, 1996.

Henri, Robert. *The Art Spirit*. New York: Basic Books, 2007.

Hess, F. Scott. "5 Artists on the Enduring Qualities of Representational Painting." *HuffPost*. December 6, 2017. https://www.huffingtonpost.com/f-scott-hess/5-artists-on-the-enduring_b_5826276.html.

Hesse, Hermann. *Steppenwolf*. New York: Picador, 2002.

"Holding On and Hoarding." Brookhaven Hospital. October 24, 2013. http://www.brookhavenhospital.com/holding-on-and-hoarding/.

"How Spiders Make Webs." Howitworksmag. June 18, 2015. https://youtu.be/e6Sq7-_G-TA.

Howarth, Eva. *Crash Course in Art*. Caldwell: Caxton Editions, 2003.

Inman, Susan. *After Her Brain Broke: Helping My Daughter Recover Her Sanity*. Dundas: Bridgeross Communications, 2010.

"Interview with John Nash: Hearing Voices." PBS. http://www.shoppbs.pbs.org/wgbh/ame/nash/sfeature/sf_nash06.html

"An Interview with Ryszard Kapuściński: Writing about Suffering," *The Journal of the International Institute* 6, no. 1 (Fall 1998). http://hdl.handle.net/2027/spo.4750978.0006.107.

Irwin, William, Mark T. Conrad and Aeon J. Skoble, eds. *The Simpsons and Philosophy: The D'oh! Of Homer.* Vol. 2. Chicago: Open Court, 2003.

Iyer, Pico. *The Art of Stillness: Adventures in Going Nowhere.* New York: Simon & Schuster/TED, 2014.

Jenkins, Roberta. "Study Examines Why Left Cheek Portraits Appear Happier." PsyPost. April 3, 2017. https://www.psypost.org/2017/04/study-examines-left-cheek-portraits-appear-happier-48654.

"Johanna van Gogh-Bonger." Wikipedia. https://en.wikipedia.org/wiki/Johanna_van_Gogh-Bonger#cite_note-3.

Julia, Isabelle, ed. *The Modern Woman: Drawings by Degas, Renoir, Toulouse-Lautrec and Other Masterpieces from the Musée D'Orsay, Paris.* Published in conjunction with an exhibition of the same title. Vancouver: Vancouver Art Gallery, 2010.

Kandinsky, Wassily. *Concering the Spiritual in Art.* New York: Dover Publications, 1977.

Kapuściński, Ryszard. *The Other.* London: Verso, 2008.

Kerouac, Jack. *On the Road.* New York: Penguin, 2011.

Kluba, William. *Where Does Art Come From? How to Find Inspiration and Ideas.* New York: Allworth, 2014.

Krznaric, Roman. *Empathy: Why It Matters, and How to Get It.* New York: TarcherPerigee, 2015.

Landau, Ellen G. *Jackson Pollock.* New York: Abrams Books, 2010.

MacKay, Sandra Yuen. *My Schizophrenic Life: The Road to Recovery from Mental Illness.* Dundas: Bridgeross Communications, 2010.

"Marcel Marceau Remembered (CBS Sunday Morning)." September 25, 2007. Video, 0:30. https://www.youtube.com/watch?v=QbxNWmH6CAo&-feature=youtu.be.

Martini, Clem, and Olivier Martini. *Bitter Medicine: A Graphic Memoir of Mental Illness.* Calgary: Freehand Books, 2010.

McNatt, Glenn. "Photography and Painting Influence Each Other." *Baltimore Sun*, February 15, 1998. https://www.baltimoresun.com/news/bs-xpm-1998-02-15-1998046086-story.html.

Meglin, Nick. *Drawing from Within: Unleashing Your Creative Potential.* Cincinatti: North Light Books, 2008.

Morrell, Peter. "Family Dynamics and the Third Child as Outsider." July 1999. http://www.homeoint.org/morrell/misc/thirdchild.htm.

Nasar, Sylvia. *A Beautiful Mind.* New York: Simon & Schuster, 1998.

Nicolaides, Kimon. *The Natural Way to Draw: A Working Plan for Art Study.* Boston: Mariner Books, 1990.

Nietzsche, Friedrich. *Thus Spoke Zarathustra: A Book for All and None.* Translated by Walter Kaufmann. Revised edition. New York: Modern Library, 1995.

Oliver, Mary. "When Death Comes." *New and Selected Poems.* Boston: Beacon Press, 1992.

Oriah, Mountain Dreamer. *What We Ache For: Creativity and the Unfolding of Your Soul.* San Francisco: HarperOne, 2005.

Peacock, Molly. *The Paper Garden: Mrs. Delany Begins Her Life's Work at 72.* Toronto: McClelland & Stewart, 2010.

Plato. *The Republic.* Bk. 7.

Powers, Ron. *No One Cares About Crazy People: The Chaos and Heartbreak of Mental Health in America.* New York: Hachette Books, 2017.

Raczka, Bob. *Name That Style: All about Isms in Art.* Minneapolis: Millbrook Press, 2009.

Reichold, Klaus, and Bernhard Graf. *Paintings That Changed the World: From Lascaux to Picasso*. Prestel, 2010.

Ross, Marvin. *Schizophrenia: Medicine's Mystery, Society's Shame*. Dundas: Bridgeross Communications, 2008.

Rumi. *The Essential Rumi*. Translated by Coleman Barks. San Francisco: Harper, 1995.

Saks, Elyn R. *The Center Cannot Hold: My Journey Through Madness*. New York: Hachette Books, 2008.

Schultz, Charles. *Peanuts*. July 13, 1954.

Shusterman, Neal. *Challenger Deep*. New York: HarperCollins, 2015.

"Spider Shoots 25 Metre Web." BBC Earth. June 25, 2017. https://youtu.be/nlRkwuAcUd4.

Sternau, Susan A. *Matisse*. New York: Todtri, 1997.

"Steve Jobs' Speech at Stanford University." Obituaries, National Public Radio. October 6, 2011. https://www.npr.org/2011/10/06/141122856/steve-jobs-speech-at-stanford-university.

Strauss, Neil. "The Pop Life: Michael Jackson's Sound of Silence." *New York Times*, December 21, 1995. https://www.nytimes.com/1995/12/21/arts/the-pop-life-michael-jackson-s-sound-of-silence.html.

"Ten Things Chris Hadfield Can't Live Without." *Toronto Life*, November 6, 2014. https://torontolife.com/city/chris-hadfield-the-list/.

Thoreau, Henry David. "Civil Disobedience." 1849. http://xroads.virginia.edu/~hyper2/thoreau/civil.html.

Tolkien, J.R.R. *The Hobbit: Or, There and Back Again*. London: HarperCollins, 2003.

Tolle, Eckhart. *A New Earth: Awakening to Your Life's Purpose*. New York: Penguin, 2005.

———. "Your Essential Nature." April 28, 2011. http://spiritualtalks.com/eckhart-tolle-your-essential-nature.

Tolstoy, Leo. *What Is Art?* Translated by Richard Pevear and Larissa Volokhonsky. London: Penguin, 1996.

Twain, Mark. *The Adventures of Tom Sawyer.* New York: Penguin, 2006.

Underwood, Raphael. "Lithium for Schizophrenia: Cochrane Find Lack of Evidence to Support Its Use." National Elf Service. https://www.nationalelfservice.net/mental-health/schizophrenia/lithium-for-schizophrenia-cochrane-find-lack-of-evidence-to-support-its-use/.

Vogler, Christopher. *The Writer's Journey: Mythic Structure for Writers.* Studio City: Michael Wiese Productions, 2007.

Waldron, Ingrid. "Communicating with a Loved One Who Has a Mental Illness." National Alliance on Mental Illness. https://namipamainline.org/communicating-with-a-loved-one-who-has-a-mental-illness/.

Walton, Julia. *Words on Bathroom Walls.* New York: Random House, 2017.

White, E.B. *Charlotte's Web.* New York: HarperCollins, 2012.

Wolfe, Tom. *The Electric Kool-Aid Acid Test.* New York: Picador, 1968.

Woods, Michael. *Drawing Basics: An Artist's Guide to Mastering the Medium.* New York: Watson-Guptill, 2000.

ACKNOWLEDGEMENTS

To Ann Webborn of the Art Studios, a.k.a. the Vancouver Recovery Through Art Society, for her unconditional support of Steve and his talent. To all the Art Studios staff and teachers, much appreciation.

To North Van Arts for embracing Steve's work in their Art Rental Programme.

To Basic Inquiry, home of the Vancouver Life Drawing Society, and to all of the Tuesday-morning artists we met over the eight years we spent there.

To Eva Bouchard of Emily Carr University of Art and Design, who helped establish the Stephen A. Corcoran Memorial Award, a first of its kind for students coping with mental illness.

To Margo Lamont of the Grind Writers, for her kindness and inclusivity, and to April Bosshard of Deep Story Design workshops. Margo calls April a "story whisperer," and I wholeheartedly agree.

To the creative non-fiction (CNF) mentorship of Jane Hamilton Silcott, whose ten-week course at UBC Writing Centre helped kick-start this project.

To my email mentor, Alessandra Naccarato, of the UBC Booming Ground Writers' Community, whose first-rate feedback helped shape an early draft.

To my friends, book club, West Vancouver Library writers-in-residence, and the North Shore Writers' Association: thank you for your sustenance.

To Vici Johnstone and the team at Caitlin Press, I offer thanks for your guidance along the way.

To my family of musketeers…we be not three, but six (2+2+2 and you), with love and new generations to gentle along.

To my husband, Ken, who has always been there for me. All my love.

JOAN BOXALL is a retired English teacher turned creative non-fiction writer. She received a bachelor's degree in physical education with an English and French major from the University of British Columbia. She taught English, French and PE to teens in Cranbrook and Delta before acquiring a TESL certificate in adult education. She contributes her non-fiction work regularly to *Inspired 55+ Lifestyle Magazine*. *DrawBridge* is her first book. She lives in North Vancouver with her husband.

Born and raised in Vancouver, STEPHEN A. CORCORAN trained at the Vancouver Art School in the 1970s (renamed Emily Carr University of Art + Design). His first solo exhibit was in February 2011 at Vancouver's Basic Inquiry Gallery. His second exhibit was at the same venue in October 2013, shortly before his death.